Swing Trading for Beginners

How to Become a Swing Trader with
Strategies, Routines, Tools
Technical Analysis for Stocks, Options and
Forex Investments, Trading Psychology,
and Money Management

By Andrew Stock

Table of Contents

Introduction

Congratulations on purchasing *Swing Trading for Beginners: How to Become a Swing Trader with Strategies, Routines, Tools. Technical Analysis for Stocks, Options and Forex Investments, Trading Psychology and Money Management* and thank you for doing so. Swing trading offers numerous benefits to several different types of investors that make it superior to more traditional forms of trading, once you get the hang of it.

It is not without its own unique quirks that can leave you broke if not handled with care, however, which is why the following chapters will discuss everything that you need to know in order to ensure that you can benefit from everything that swing trading has to offer. The benefits of swing trading cannot be underestimated. Over the years, many people have chalked tremendous success in swing trading. There literally thousands and millions of people out there who have greatly benefited from swing trading. With that said, I'm humbled to inform you that you've made the right choice to start swing trading.

As with every game, there are rules. The rules determine the tone and manner for which the game is played. The better you understand and stick with the rules of the game, the more you will enjoy swing trading and do well. You have to understand that the primary reason many people fail in swing trading is that, they try to jump the learning curve.

There's a learning curve in anything. To be excellent at swing trading, it is very important that you learn the rules that promise and assures success in swing trading. I get it, there are investors who do not want anything to do with the market. Therefore, they seek and look out for venture capitalist to help fund their projects.

The exciting thing about swing trading is the sheer fact that you get to trade with various financial instruments: from stocks, options, mutual funds, index funds, currencies, cryptos, and many others. With many trading opportunities available, you can just look for the variation between upswings and downswings to make good trading decisions that earn profits.

With the help of technical and fundamental indicators, you can begin to find entry and exit points to trade. Swing trading is a short term strategy to earn profits in the financial market. That means with intelligent analysis and speculation, you can start earning profits as high as 20% in just a week of engaging in trade. There are always various technical tools and indicators to help make the right trading decisions.

When it comes to education and experience, you can say that you've got all it. No matter how much you know, there is still a lot to learn. You can still learn more, know more and get more experience as you trade. The nicer part about swing trading is that the more you educated and experience you become, the more money you make in the trade.

You can look for tips, articles, ebooks, podcasts, videos, and many others to advance your knowledge. This book is just one of them. Once you gain knowledge, you need the courage to put them into practice and get the required results. As you practice what you learn over time, you will begin to get consistent wins and profits which will grow your portfolio. Enjoy your reading!

Chapter One: Swing Trading Overview

"Swing trading is a short-term stock trading style. You take smaller profits, cut losses quicker, and hold stocks for less time."
~Justin Nielson

If you have a considerable amount of passion, knowledge and trading capital, you can do well in the financial market. Many people have seen the tremendous potential of the financial market to enable them to generate extra income that helps to achieve their financial future. The fact is that the financial market is very wide and big and you have to develop a good strategy to play in the game.

While we've been hearing stories of many millionaire traders who did very well in the market, there are many other people who run into huge losses. If you want to succeed in the financial market, you have to develop a trading plan and then use that plan as a yardstick to guide all trading activities.

Generally speaking, you can either be a trader or an investor. Even though both traders and investors play in the same market, they do it differently. Warren Buffett, the Oracle of Omaha has been recognized as the richest and most successful investor of all time. George Soros is also a success in the stock market, but he plays the game in a different way.

Usually, investors have a long term view. This could be a year, a decade or three decades. They analyze and evaluate a stock, buy the stock and hold the position for a very long time to collect dividends. The game of the investor is dividends. Investors want to compound their monetary value over a long term period. Therefore, they evaluate a company, buy their stock and hold it for many years. The investor is not worried about the rise and fall of a stock price. The main income-generating stream of the investor is an inflow of annual dividends.

There is another way of playing the game. Instead of buying a position in a company and then holding it for years to collect a dividend, you can choose to buy the position at a lower price and then sell it at a higher price to make a profit. This form of playing in the financial market is known as trading because it focuses on buying securities at one price and then selling them at another price to make a profit. The accumulated profit over a long period of time tends to yield a greater return. This is where many people are entering the financial market.

Today, millions of people are becoming security traders by learning about volatility, price trends, and patterns in the market and how to play the game to win. The securities traded in the financial market include options, stocks, index, commodities, futures, and currencies. Each financial instrument varies from the other, therefore, the trader needs to learn and understand the fundamentals of each market and the best way to approach. Once you get to know the securities and where you want to focus your time and attention, you need to then develop a trading style. This is where swing trading, trending trading, day trading, scalp trading, and all others come in.

Three Kinds of Traders

There are various levels f traders in the financial market: beginner, intermediate and advanced. Your knowledge, experience, and profits over time enable you to determine your level of trading ability. Most brokers would want to know your level of trading to enable them customized offering to meet your needs. Thus, before you learn about the swing trading overview, you might want to look at the three kinds of traders in the financial market and know where you belong.

Beginner Traders

A beginner trader in the financial market is looking for ways and means to make a profit in the market by minimizing losses and without risking so much investment capital. Many beginner traders, today, prefer options trading because of the flexibility of enabling them to own options to buy particular security without bearing the risk of buying it upfront. Many of these beginner traders have their own jobs, buy study and learn about the financial market to develop a second stream of income through capital gains.

Intermediate Traders

These people have a certain amount of experience and knowledge in the financial market. They understand the game and have a way of analyzing securities. The intermediate traders may trade stocks, commodities, and options. They know how the market works, understand how to time the market and have made a considerable amount of wins in the market. The intermediate trader may not be the one with the millionaire portfolio account to manage, but they are people how to understand and know what they are doing.

Advanced Traders

These are the professional traders with sophisticated methods, strategies, and schemes of analyzing the market developed through years of trading activities. They manage a high amount of money in their portfolio, therefore, they seem to take much more calculated risks than the intermediate or the beginner traders. Some of these advanced traders may engage in day trading or even trend trading for a while. They are professionals who even trade full time in the financial market, either for themselves or on the behalf of their clients.

What is Swing Trading?

Swing Trading is one of the trading styles used by traders to make profits in the financial market by taking advantage of the price volatility of an asset. It focuses on how to capture immediate profits in the stock market or any financial market by analyzing the price "swing" of an underlying asset. Swing traders need to be skillful at studying trends, patterns, and direction of the price of securities and then making good predictions on where it is likely to go next.

A long term stock trader may use a long position in a stock to make bigger profits over a period of time. But, as a swing trader, that is not your preoccupation. You are looking to make profits in the financial market by looking for what is known as "potential price move" and then "capturing gains in the market" based on various technical indicators. Usually, most swing traders may choose to hold positions in an underlying stock for a few days, weeks or even a month.

Types of Swing Traders

All types of trading styles involve the use of technical and fundamental analysis to analyze stock price movement and then entering the market to capture profits based on key indicators. Even though swing trading focuses on making a profit by capitalizing on an impending, sharp change in stock, there are two types of swing trading methods.

1. *Short Term Swing Trading:*

In this case, the holding time for a swing trader is a couple of days. It may be two days of three days. The swing trader is looking for an opportunity to capture some profits in the marketplace by analyzing the price volatility, trend, and direction of stocks in the financial market. A short term swing trader may focus on analyzing the market by reading daily or 60-minute charts.

Apart from the time frame for the swing trading being short, many of these traders seem to hold a smaller position. For example, a trader may choose to swing a stock for $ 34 with only 200 shares. Due to the risks associated with some of these short term trading techniques, many traders tend to hold smaller positions while looking to maximize gains through sudden price fluctuations.

2. Long Term Swing Trading:

In this swing trading, the focus is a little bit wider than just a couple of days. The swing trader is looking to make money in the price swing of an underlying asset over a week or more. The trader studies and analyze the financial market using daily and weekly charts. This enables them to have a long term perspective about the market and then know when to enter and exit.

A swing trader can decide to trade for the short term and also for the long term. There are no hard and fast rules about it. Swing trading generally involves finding ways to make shorter or immediate term profits by finding sudden, potential price changes in the stock market of publicly traded companies. Generally. Swing traders are either intra-day, intra-week or even intra-month stock traders. The focus is not about the holding time but finding the entry and exit points on a stock price movement to capture profits.

The Basic Concepts of Swing Trading

Once you settle on swing trading, you need to have a good overview of swing trading and how it works to do well in the long term. Your knowledge of swing trading and how to play to win in the game will give a greater edge in the financial market. As they say, " To a man with a hammer everything is a nail." As long as you study the swing trading and the fundamentals, you can apply the swing trading strategies and techniques to any kind of stock, option, or financial instrument. To be successful in swing trading, you need to develop the mindset and thought patterns of the successful traders.

When you see how the game works, you can plan how to make the move to ensure most of your swing trading moves yields better results: The following are the basic concepts you have to keep in mind when executing any swing trading strategy:

1. *Use technical and fundamental analysis to look for price trends, directions, and movements of stocks so that tactical plans can be put in place to know when to make a move.* This forms the basis for selecting the right stocks for swing trading. Success in swing trading has a lot to do with picking and selecting the right stocks from the beginning.

2. *Identifying the stock market and looking for where the price of a particular stock is most likely to move in the next few days or weeks.* Entry and exit points are crucial in swing trading. There is a time to enter and exit the market to capture the profit. That is why timing and regular market monitoring of the market is very important.

3. *Making Risk/Reward Ratio Analysis.* Before each swing trade movement is made, a seasoned swing trader wants to know what amount of risk should be borne and what amount of reward can be reaped from the trading activity. This helps in using mechanisms such as stop loss and profit target for better trading experience.

4. *Entering the market by buying a position of a stock with a potential price swing movement in the near future to yield a considerable amount of profit.* Once stock and risk/reward analysis has been done, a specific swing trading strategy can be executed to ensure the best outcome is obtained from the underlying trading activity.

5. *Holding the position for the short term. It can be a couple of days or weeks and then looking for where a surge in stock price is likely to take place.* Regular monitoring and analysis of the stock market to get an update on the underlying position are very important for a successful swing trading.

6. *Capturing profits and gains from stock price movement.* The game of swing trading is looking for avenues to make immediate gains by looking at the volatility and price and trend of an underlying stock. Once the market moves, profits can be realized by

making a swing through selling a position to make profits from the trading activity.

7. *Evaluating the trade and profit/loss made.* A good swing trader wants to learn from every single trade and improve the application of strategies and techniques over a period of time. After each trade, either a win or loss, the successful swing trader wants to evaluate and study the trade to glean lessons which would be used to make the next trade very successful.

8. *Moving unto the next trading opportunity.* A swing trader analyzes the market to find entry and exit points, captures profit through the swing and then moves on to the next trading opportunity. There is no need worrying or brawling about a position that has been lost due to missed predictions and analysis. You move to the next trading opportunity.

The whole concept of trading is about buying and selling to make a profit. You buy low, sell high and then make a profit. You can also sell a position before the market price of that security goes down in value so that you can profit from a downward market. To do very well trading in the financial market, you have to decide on the security and the trading style you want to use to play the game.

What Makes Swing Trading So Popular?

Swing trading has taken on a nosedive in recent times. Many people are taking advantage of swing trading due to their flexibility, profit/loss structure and the minimum amount of engagement required to be successful in the trade.

While all the three types of traders can engage in swing trading, it seems to be a favorable and suitable medium for beginner traders. Both intermediate and advanced traders can use swing trading to increase the value of their portfolio, but swing trading seems to be suitable for beginner or non-active traders.

Swing trading does not involve keen oversight and insight into the financial market to make profits. It involves holding positions for a few days or weeks to make a profit. Regular feedback and monitoring are needed to do well in swing trading. Nonetheless, with just a couple of hours per day, any individual can start studying the financial market and get started with swing trading.

To do well in swing trading, you need to dedicate regular and ongoing time for studying the market. The more you study the market, the better your insight about what is going on and the ability to predict trends to capture quick profits in the market. The game of swing trading is all about knowing where the market is going and then finding ways and means to capitalize on that move and make short term profits.

Even though there are risks associated with swing trading, it is less time consuming and engaging as compared to other trading styles. If you're looking to start trading in the stock market, swing trading is one the best ways to get in the game. As compared to day traders who need to have a deeper understanding of various technical and fundamental indicators that influence the price of a security, you don't have to worry too much about these times. With just a couple of hours per day and a trading capital, you can start with swing trading.

Chapter Two: Is Swing Trading Right for Me?

"A common method for distinguishing one type of trader from another is the time period for which a trader holds a stock—a variance which can range from a few seconds to months or even years."
~Prableen Bajpai

If you are looking to make some money in the stock or any other financial market, there are various ways of doing that. Even though swing trading has become a popular trading style of the majority, you have to analyze yourself and see if swing trading is right for you.

The punchline is that you don't have to follow the masses and do what everyone else is doing. You need to do a good analysis of yourself and choose a trading style that works best for you. It should come from a good analysis of your trading & exit plan and your temperament. There are various trading styles you can adopt to increase the value of your portfolio in the stock market.

But you need to make sure what you have chosen meets your personality, temperament, knowledge, experience and trading plan. If you choose what works best for you, it will ease of trading and moving forward even when the going gets tough. You need to understand the level of emotional intelligence required to be successful with each trading style.

Typically, investors always want to hold the position of stock for years and decades. These people tend to be "emotionally immune" to stock price fluctuations in the market. They don't really care about the interest rates and the demand forces increasing or decreasing the value of their stock holdings. They look to the company which sold the stock to generate returns for their investments. They learn to stay calm and be emotionally stable in an upward market and a downward market.

On the other hand, if you are looking to get into day trading, swing trading or even trend trading, you need to watch your emotions. Temperament and emotional intelligence play a big role in being successful with any trading style. If you are fearful and risk-averse, you might be looking for a more safer trading style that meets your personality.

Also, if you are risk-tolerant and risk-loving, you might want to look for a trading style that will maximize your strength. Whichever way, you need to make sure you look at the downside of each trading opportunity before making a move. Always try to make sure you know an understand the trading style you want to use and how it matches with your goals, plans, and aspirations.

Types of Trading

There are various types of trading styles to adopt when you are looking to trade in the financial market. In fact, you can get drowned by these many trading styles and techniques. Therefore, it is advisable that you, first of all, develop a succinct and clear trading plan that outlines your profit target and a plan to achieve that goal. It will also be good to clarify the timeline for your investment. Your plan should also detail the kind of security you want to deal with and then your temperamental approach to the general financial market.

Once you've got to your plane ready, it is time to take a helicopter view of major types of trading styles and then look for the one that best fits your plan and trading personality. Beware that you need to make sure you use a trading style that guarantees an X amount of profit but rather what will make you successful in your trading in the financial market.

Even though other trading styles may exist in between, there are three main types of trading to look at when you are considering settling a trading methodology to develop and grow your investment portfolio in the financial market" day trading, swing trading and position trading.

Day Trading

As the name implied, day trading simply means a financial trading style that does not get overnight. A day trading lasts only for a day. Traders are looking for volatile stocks they are observing or experiencing price movements to ensure that they achieve a considerable amount of success. Usually, day trading lasts from a few seconds to hours in the day.

The trading session closes with the close of each business day. Traders do not get the chance to hold their financial positions overnight. These are where many options, volatile stocks, currencies, and commodity trading comes. To be successful as a day trader, you need to have a keen eye on the market and mapping the trend and price patterns of financial securities.

You need to also be very good in the use of technical analysis to forecast and predict new price movements in the financial market to be able to earn a substantial amount of profit. You also want to make sure you know how to read the daily charts, 60-minutes charts, 30-minutes charts and all other charts to gain better insight into the securities in the marketplace.

Swing Trading

While day trading expires after each business day, swing trading continues for days and even several weeks. You can say that the next step in the time horizon ladder of trading is the swing trading. The time structure in this trading style reveals the fact theta the underlying financial security will have to take time before experiencing a swing in stock price to realize a profit.

Some swing traders who seem to be fundamental analysis inclined realizes that when the underlying company makes corporate changes or alterations, it may take a few days or weeks for it to reflect on the price of the stock. Therefore, a swing trader needs to read the stock trends and patterns and also follow the fundamental news to gain better insight into when and how the stock price might go up in order to experience a profit on the trade.

Swing trading involves more than one trading session. By analyzing the profit trend of the stock, you get to know when and how to make moves in the stock market in order to realize a profit. The main focus in swing trading is to keep an eye on a trend of stock price direction and make profits when the movement experiences a sudden change.

Position Trading

While day trading and swing trading deals with the now, position trading deals with the future. People who use position trading style buy and hold for a long period of time, expecting that the value of other stock holdings will increase with passing time. Well, while this can yield substantial profits when the underlying stock or financial instrument experiences an increase in shareholder value over time. Position traders may decide to hold their position for several months and years until they have attained their desired target profit where they think they can move on.

Long term investors are known for their ability to buy and hold for several years. After long term investors, position traders tend to be the next group on the line with the ability to buy and hold stocks for a long period of time to yield the desire share per price value. They operate with the belief that when the trend starts, it will continue for a long period of time. Based on this belief, they lunch their position trader style which yields good returns based on the trend and direction of the stock over time.

Position traders are usually passive when it comes to stock trading; they buy one stock and then hold it for a long time until it yields the maximum results where they choose to sell their position and move unto the next thing. But to do well in position trading, it requires that carefully fundament and technical analysis to be made before taking the hit. If price reversal takes place, position traders may lose a high value of their stock or financial asset's value.

Day Trading, Swing Trading or Position Trading - A Comparative Analysis

Having understood the three styles of trading in the financial market, which is best of you? Which meets your goals, dreams, plans and personality style? Which will best work for you in attaining your portfolio dreams and profit margins? Before you consider making any decision, you need to know that all the three types of trading styles have the potential to generate a huge profit over time.

If you trade conservatively and wisely for a period of time, you are most likely to make more money in the market either you have been using day trading, swing trading or position trading. It is also very important that there is no free lunch in security trading. There are risks involved in any trade. You must do your risk/reward analysis before taking any trade decision.

Always endeavor to trade what you can lose. While the margin is good to use in stock or financial trading, you might jeopardize your financial life if you take all your money and bet it all on one stock. Make sure you have done your analysis and taken a considerable amount of time to shield your profits from much loss.

Now, let's take a closer look at how the three trading styles work and compare with each other, consider the following in-depth analysis. Knowing the difference in the trading approach will know what you need to do well and how you should strategize to excel in any type of trading style.

Day Trading

- Frequency of Trading: trading positions are held for minutes or hours on a business day. Traders can profit from trading financial securities by trading highly volatile stocks that will fluctuate on a working day to generate a profit on share per profit. Keeping track of multiple portfolios can become a challenge of the day trader.

- Commitment: Generally, day trading involves more commitment than any other form of trading style. The lower the time frame of the asset to increase or depreciate in value, the higher the monitoring and feedback required to make a win in the market. This can increase stress levels when other responsibilities are involved.

- Trading Method: If you choose to use a day trading method to play the game of the financial market, then you need to be actively engaged in the management of your portfolio. Day traders are highly immersed in the game, they follow the market and trend to make a good trading decision. They focus on buying or selling highly volatile stocks so that they can make profits.

- Liquidity: For those using a day trading method, you need to be liquid. As a day trader, every day is a trading day, but you can choose to place an order for a trading decision if you want. When you are day trader, you're liquid since you sell positions to make profits. Buying and selling are done daily, therefore your money is locked up in a stock or any other financial security.

- Trading Expenses: Generally, the shorter the trading time frame, the higher the trading expenses and the accompanying profit to be made in the trade. In a day trading, you are required to get all the financial data to make buying and selling decisions. That means bearing costs such as trading charts, insider trading news, brokerage commissions and paying for ongoing trade alerts.

- Leverage & Start-Up Costs: Usually day trading have high start-up costs, but you get to use leverage to maximize returns for each individual trade. By contacting your broker, you can get access to a host of margin that can be used to increase the return on each trading session. But you need to aware of the risks associated with margin.

- Competition: Many top-notch traders like the hedge funds and sophisticated trading institutions using computer program tend to play the day trading game. These people have a lot of cash at disposal, spending millions of dollars to manage multiply portfolio. As a day trader, you will be competing with these organizations in trading. Using smart tools and strategies is important to excel in the game.

- Risk Analysis: Sometimes, the stock price may fail to move or change as implied by the financial media and this could lead to potential losses in trading. A day trader might be exposed to a lot of risk in options trading when the option does not have enough time value to get "in the money" and earn profits from the trade.

Swing Trading

Frequency of Trading: Swing trading generally involves a short time frame, a couple of days and weeks of holding and selling stock positions. Due to the low frequency of trading as compared to day trading, many corporate executives and buy professionals or beginner traders tend to enter the market through this trading outlet.

Commitment: Even though you get to place several trades in a month, you need a considerable amount of commitment to excel as a swing trader. To do well in swing trader, it is very important to invest an hour or so to study the financial market, especially the stock market. You need regular daily or weekly monitoring some few minutes of the day through charts and platforms to stay on top of the game.

Trading Method: The aim of the swing trader is to identify the next move in stock prices, and then capitalize on the move to earn huge profits. Thus, the swing trader seeks to find volatile stocks, but the position and hold it for a couple of days or weeks, sell the position and earn profit from the price variance. Swing traders make money when they sell, but expend money when they buy positions.

Liquidity: As a swing trader, you may not be as liquid as a day trader. Since the trading activities are done either within the week or month, your funds may be locked up in your brokerage account while awaiting the underlying stock or financial security to swing for profit maximization. Having funds to take advantage of new stocks with potential price swings is very important.

Trading Expenses: A swing trader is not engaged in day to day trading activities, therefore there is not enough monitoring of the market. Most of the charts used by swing traders are free and involves only minutes of checking or monitoring to stay on track with the market. This is why swing trading seems to be favorable for beginner traders in the stock, commodity, and Forex trading market.

Leverage & Start-Up Costs: As compared with day trading, swing trading involves less trading capital to get started. Most swing traders tend not to very active with the management of their positions, requiring less trading capital to make swings and profits in the game. However, there are leverage packages with brokerage firms for swing traders; amounts provided may be as much as those involved in swing trading.

Competition: Swing trading does not involve a high barrier of entry and stiff competition like the day traders. Notwithstanding, there is an amount of tracking, analysis, and evaluation required to place any trader. There might also be competition regarding the trading of a particular stock as well as the market conditions regarding the volume of the stock.

Risk Analysis: Stock prices can change overnight and result in losses. This is why it is very important to take a closer look at the financial position of a stock or any financial instrument before placing a trade. Always make sure you do the required technical and fundamental analysis before swinging a trade.

Position Trading

Frequency of Trading: Position trading involves a long term perspective. You are not thinking of the next swing or change in prices to make a profit. Position traders buy and hold for a long period of time until their stock holdings increase in value. The time frame for position trading may be in months and even years, as long as it takes to reach the expected to earn potential of stock before selling.

Commitment: Position traders are the most passive traders. While day trading requires more activity in terms of constant monitoring and watching live stock price fluctuations to make a better trading decision, a position trader may check the charts and market status from time to time. There may be ongoing technical and fundamental analysis to make evaluation prior to a trade, but not as involving as a day trader.

Trading Method: Position traders buy and hold for a very long time and then sell when they have reached the expected profit-earning per share or when the market is expecting a huge change. Their trading philosophy requires that they don't worry about daily price changes of an underlying security, but rather make money from the long term valuation and price trend following.

Liquidity: A day trader sells and buys positions daily to earn profits, but a position trader has to wait for a long period of time before cashing in. After a position trader buys a position of the stock, the trading capital will be locked in for a period of time the trader is awaiting the appreciating of the stock to sell and realize the capital gains.

Trading Expenses: As a position trader, you place only a few trades per year. Therefore, your expenses are limited. You don't get to bear the costs of paying for constant changes in prices of securities to make a profit. Usually, the position trader focuses on making profits using a long term approach, this lowest amount paid in commissions and portfolio management as compared to swing and day trading.

Leverage & Start-Up Costs: To be successful in position trading, you have to make sure that you have cash available for other things. Your trading capital may be locked up one stock for a long period of time. This is why it is important to analyze and look at your financial capabilities before using a position trading style to make profits in the stock market.

Competition: As compared to swing and day trading, there is a relatively low amount of competition in position trading. You look at various publicly traded stocks in the financial market, you take your time to do the underlying technical and fundamental analysis and then buy the stock. You hold the position and sell when everything turns green or to minimize losses in a down market.

Risk Analysis: The main risk in position trading is when the wind moves against you. When there is price reversal and the market moves contrary to your prediction, you might suffer losses. However, you can use a protective put option to protect the downside when your high earning stock seems to be going down in value.

Swing Trading: Speculation or Investment?

In his book, Security Analysis, Benjamin Graham made a clear distinction between investing and speculation. To do well in the financial market, you have to know the difference between these two practices and know when to speculate and when to invest.

For those looking to go into swing trading, understanding these two approaches to the financial market is very important to minimize your loss and maximize your gains.Benjamin Graham said, " *An investment operation is one which, upon thorough analysis promises the safety of the principle and an adequate return. Operations not meeting these requirements are speculative.*"

When Warren Buffet was asked the difference between investing and speculation, these were his words: *"An investment operation in my view is one where you look at the asset itself to determine your decision to lay out some money now to get some more money back later on. So you look to the apartment, house, you look to the stock, you look to the farm in terms of what that will produce. And you don't really care whether there's a quote under it at all. You are basically committing some funds now to get more funds later on through the operation of the asset.*

Speculation, I would define, as much more focused on the price action of the stock, particularly that you buy or the indexed future or something of the sort. Because you are not really, you are counting on, for whatever factors, could be quarterly earnings, could be up or it's going to split or whatever it may be or increase the dividend, but you are not looking to the asset itself.

And I say the real test of how you, what you're doing is whether you care whether the markets are open. When I buy a stock, I don't care whether they close the stock market tomorrow or for a couple of years... Now if I care whether the stock market is open tomorrow then I say to some extent I'm speculating because I'm thinking about whether the price is going to go up tomorrow or now. And then gambling I would define as engaging in a transaction which doesn't need to be part of the system..."

With that said, speculation involves is about trading. Buying a stock and hoping it increases in value so that you can sell it to make a profit. Whereas investing is buying a stock and then expecting the stock to generate returns to you in a form of annual dividends. You can invest in a stock without the stock market telling you changing prices and quotes.

Speculation, on the other hand, deals with using the financial market information to make intelligent security analysis and trading decision. Swing Trading is a form of speculation. But just as there is intelligent investing, there is intelligent speculation. If you trade based on technical and fundamental indicators, you will reduce your risks, trade intelligently and increase the returns on your trading activities. If you do it well, you'll be massively successful.

Chapter Three: Setting Up & Choosing a Broker

"Picking your broker is not much different from picking a stock. It starts with knowing your investing style. And today you have more options than earlier generations could dream of."

~ Brian Beers

The game of swing trading is pretty straight forward. To get started with swing trading there are a couple of things that you need to make sure are in place. Getting a trading capital and setting up a brokerage account for your financial security trading is the chiefest amount the list of things to do. Even though these things are important, always ensure you invest in your trading education.

The more educated you are in swing trading and related strategies to win in the game, the better your chances of doing well in the long term. You see, the fact is that you don't want to waste both time and capital and finally end up being wiped out of the game. Therefore, always take your education, knowledge and personal investment seriously.

Remember what Warren Buffet said, " The more you learn, the more you earn." The more you learn about swing trading, strategies and methods of successful traders, the more successful you will also become in the trade. Read books, attend a conference, join forums, read the newspapers, read books, subscribe for swing trading magazines, consult the experts, read industry-related articles and all others.

Just make sure you are learning and upgrading yourself. Once you realized that you have a fair understanding of how swing trading works and how to win in the game, start the process of putting together a risk capital for the options. You can't trade in options with just margin: what amount of personal capital are you bringing on board? What amount of leverage do you want to employ in your trading activities?

Determine Your Risk Capital

There are two main things you have to know here: your risk capital and the overall trading capital. Your trading capital is the total amount of money that you have set aside to invest, trade and speculate on financial instruments. It can be the minimum amount of deposit required by your broker to start trading using their platform. It could also be a certain of money in your bank or savings account that you have personally dedicated to your trading activities.

What then is your risk capital? As the name suggests, the risk capital is the amount of a trading capital set aside for speculative trading activities in the financial market. When you are dealing with a venture, the meaning might slightly change. In that regard, the risk capital is the amount of money required to invest in a promising, but an unproven venture with the expectation of getting more returns in the future.

Risk capital is very important in options trading. You want to know how much you can afford to lose in all your trading activities. Whether you are investing or speculating, there's going to be an amount of risk. The risk here means the possibility of losing your money. Therefore, you need to make sure you understand the risks associated with each trade before committing any amount of money into the trade.

Your risk capital is the amount of money that you can afford to lose on a trade. Many industry experts say that a risk capital of 10% of your overall trading capital is good.
In general, if you are risk-averse, you need to make sure that you start small and then increase your risk capital as you go along. You don't want to expose yourself to too much risk. Conduct a risk/reward analysis to know the amount of risk involved in a trade and decide whether you can afford to take the risk and bear the chances of losing your money should the market fail to go as expected.

Seasoned traders who have had years of wisdom and experience in financial trading activities tend to open themselves to a high amount of risk. They know the game, the trade and how everything works. Their knowledge, which becomes instinctive for them, guide their trading activities, providing them with a high analytical vision into the market. The more risk-tolerant you are, the more you might want to increase your risk capital. This can be around 15% to 25%.

Consult with your broker. Some brokers have various levels of trading activities which limits the individual amount of money to risk for a trade. Your broker can also advise and guide to make a good decision on the amount of risk capital to commit to your trade. Be clear about your level of experience and knowledge of security trading and then decide the amount of money to commit.

Choosing a Broker

After you've decided on your risk capital, the next thing you have to consider is your broker. Your broker is like your trading partner. The type of broker you choose for your trading activities can either make or break you. Therefore, don't take this decision lightly. Many amateur traders simply choose any type of broker for their portfolio management. But, that is the best decision to take.

You should always make sure you put in a great deal of thought into selecting a broker. A good broker will completely enhance your trader and enable you to achieve your desired target. A good broker sees you as their partner and their client. Their financial success depends on your success in trading. Hence, they provide all kinds of platforms and resources to make sure your trading activities yield a higher return on investment.

When you a considering the kind of broker to choose, there are a lot of things that come to mind. Even though there are many factors to consider when selecting a broker for your portfolio management, the following should be a key determining factor:

1. Trading opportunities offered
2. Account fees
3. Commissions on trading
4. Minimum account deposit
5. Trading levels & tech support
6. Trading incentives & promotions

Trading Opportunities Offered

This is probably the first thing you should look at when choosing a broker for your trading activities. Don't assume that all brokers offer the same investment opportunities. There are various brokers for various groups. What you need to do is to make sure you know and understand your trading plan and style, then select the best investment opportunities that meet it.

What do you want to trade-in? Is it options, stocks, index, futures, commodities, currencies, cryptocurrencies? Be clear on what you want to trade-in and then find the best brokers with the tools, resources and support system to be successful in that trade. If you are looking to trade in stocks and options, then you have to find a broker that provides the best resources at the most affordable price possible to meet your trading goals and needs.

Account Set-Up

Brokerage firms make money by managing your trading account. In doing that, they provide various services and related charges for each level of account management. While there are general account management fees like annual fees and transfer fees, you need to make sure you read and know all the various account management fees offered by the broker.

If you want to transfer your profits from your trading account to your bank account, your broker will charge a small fee to initiate the transfer. Ensure you know about these petty charges. When closing your account, you might also be charged a fee. Trading subscription and research report fees are another kind of trading fee to keep watch of.

Commissions on Trading

Commissions are another place to keep an eye on. Brokers charge a commission per trade that you place through their platform. These charges are very small that many traders simply ignore them. But, the flip side is that when you sum all the commission fees for a month and year, you'll notice that it is really a lot of money.

You're paying the broker a commission per trade, therefore make sure you know the charges before placing the trade. You don't want a broker to be pickpocketing your account through commission fees. Read the broker's pricing chart to know what they charge. There are various commissions charged per investment opportunity. Check what the broker charges in commissions for common stocks, currencies, options, EFTs, bonds and mutual funds. Look for commission-free trades, if the selected broker has that brokerage package.

Minimum Account Deposit

Brokers use the account minimum to ensure that traders fund their trading account with a sufficient amount of cash for their trading activities. Your broker wants to make sure that you don't leave your trading account bear and empty and this is the reason many brokers request minimum account deposit to commence trading.

Research various brokers based on minimum account deposit. How much do they require you to commit to your trading account when you sign up for an account? Find out the amount and then check whether you have that amount of funds ready.

While minimum account deposits vary, many brokers seem to request $ 500 and upward, based on the level of account. If you don't want a broker with a minimum account deposit, you can check brokers such as Ally Invest and Merrill Edge.

Trading Levels & Technical Support

There are various types of trading platforms: beginner, intermediate and advanced trading platforms. You need to inform the trader when opening the account about your trading experience and the type of platform you need. If you're just starting swing trading, you might want to consider a beginner trading to help with your trading activities.

Each trading platform will provide essentials such as trading tools, research, security updates, educational resources, and all others. Make sure you read the broker tech support information to know the various support services that will be provided to enable you to achieve the goal you want. Some broker charge extras for some of these additional services, so be careful to make sure you read everything carefully and know the costs associated with these technical support services of each level of the trading platform.

Trading Incentives & Promotions

What are the trading incentives provided by the broker? Some brokers provide promotional campaign which comes with surprising discounts, bonuses and free offers to incentivize traders to place more trades and earn better profits. Check out the offers that the broker provides and see how beneficial it will be for your trading activities.

You need to make sure you also look at hidden costs. You're not looking at hidden cost promos that will end up increasing the commissions per trade in the future and wipe out your trading capital. Always study and analyze the promo carefully before engaging in it. Just because the broker offers a price discount or promo does not mean you should take advantage of it. Look at the downsides of the promo and then weigh it against the benefits before making the trading decision.

Setting Up Your Trading Account

Technology has made brokerage account easy with online apps and websites. Opening a trading account is pretty simple. The steps may vary, but the following will be required for opening any type of account.

1. Provide Personal Information: These are the personal details of the trader to be used for trading account set up. Ensure you provide correct and accurate personal information which include legal name, address, email address, social security number and much more.
1. Provide Trading Information: Your broker wants to customized services to meet your needs and demands. Therefore, provide accurate information to the trader when signing about your level of education and experience in the underlying trade that you want to undertake.
2. Provide Signature: Once all details required for account opening are provided, your broker will want to sign via a digital media to append your acceptance of their policies and standards and to grant them the permission to manage your trading portfolio. You can take the time to read the contract document and know what it entails.
3. Sign up for the trading account: Once everything is ready, proceed to sign up and then review your account. Look through the trading platform to ensure that all the details required for a successful training are included in the package they told you about.

After you've settled on the best broker for your swing trading, you have to open your brokerage account. All your swing trading activities will be done through your brokerage account. Therefore, it is important that you open and set up your trading account.

Chapter Four: Fixing Your Mindset

"Being able to day trade for a living successfully means reaching a level of excellence that most people will never achieve, no matter what career they choose. It's the difference between being a movie extra and an Oscar-winning actor."
~Brian Lund

To do well in every business, you need to develop the right mindset. With the right mindset, you can swift through the challenges of everyday life and be successful in the long term. As with all businesses, the same it is with swing trading. The most successful swing traders have a winning mindset which enables them to adapt and learn along the journey and be eventually successful.

It takes time and patience to develop the right mindset for swing trading, but it is always worth it. The fact is that most people quit before they win in the game and the main reason they quit before they hit the big win is that they don't have the right mindset. You need to understand that swing trading is not easy. Every move takes risk and courage.

You need to be willing to fail, makes mistakes, learn from the mistakes and then work your plan. You have to learn how to manage risks and how to carefully navigate your course to avoid being wiped out in the trade. For those of you, looking to trade stocks for a living, you have to know that the rules of successful trading are different from the rules of successful employment.

Swing Trading for a Living

When you are employed by a traditional boss, you are given a job description. You do your job and get paid what you have done. You also get to risk sick leave, bonus and pension plan for your retirement. If you quit your job for swing trading, you need to know that you will be losing the perks that come with having a job with a corporate body.

The rules for success are not the same. You can be a successful employee at an organization, but the mindset and the training required for you to do very well is not the same trading in stocks. You need to learn and readjust your strategy and mindset if you're going to survive and thrive in swing trading. Always see yourself as being in the business of swing trading as compared to adopting an employee mentality.

According to experts, many traders lose money in the long term. To be on the other side of the game, among the successful traders who buy big houses, drive nice cars and build an amazingly wonderful portfolio, making at least six-figure income each year, you need to know and understand the tricks of the game to succeed.

 Instead of blindly quitting your job and then going straight into swing trading, the best strategy will be to keep your day time job, swing the market and gain the skillset and experience of professional traders. With the newly develop mindset, skillset, and experience, you will be in a better position to begin earning a steady stream of income, regardless of minor trade losses to do well in the game.

The following tips will guide you on starting and building your own swing trading business:

1. Have Savings Set Aside

Before you get started, make sure you have at least 6 months to one-year living expenses in cash. Yes, you need at least 6 months to one-year living expenses in cash. Some of you might be saying that's just too much. Well, it might be true! But the fact is that if you don't have enough savings aside to serve as a cushion against unforeseen circumstances, you will find yourself worrying about money for everyday life and that will take your mind off the game and kill you alive.

2. Start Small and Learn

A typical mistake of many people is putting much of their risk capital into one trade. You have to learn to diversify your trade strategy and trading activities to offset losses in the long term. Build and develop a trading plan that is consistent with your trading style and personality and then use that as a framework to start small and learn as you progress.

3. Set a Monthly Income Target

If you want to do swing trading for a living, then your goal needs to be to have a regular, predictable stream of income that covers all your living expenses with enough surplus set aside for long term investing. How much do you need for your monthly living expenses? Based on that amount, you can then plan and develop a strategy to achieve revenue and profit goals.

4. Develop a Winning Process for Trading

Once you have set your revenue goal, you have to develop a winning process to use to achieve the set target for each month. Even though you need an amount of luck to do well in swing trading, you have to make sure you develop a predictable, winning process for analyzing trades, placing trades and evaluating performance. Instead of basing trading on happenstance, have a steady winning system to manage all your trading activities.

5. Be Cautions and Careful With Everything

Sometimes, when everything is going your way and you are getting many wins per trade, you can forget to take caution. Swing trading involves risk and you can risk blowing off all your trading capital in a split second. Therefore, you need to be conservative with your trade. Analyze and access the amount of risk you are exposing yourself to before engaging in any kind of trade.

6. Focus on one market at a time

Some people want to be trading in forex, stocks, options and any other financial instrument at the same time. That will not work. You have to keep your trading efforts and energy in one single market. If you want to do well in stocks, focus on stock trading. If you want to do well in EFT, stay focus on EFT. If you want to ensure you do well in options, then focus. Successful focus on one market and become an expert at one time before moving to another.

7. **Aim at Being Excellent**

Brain Lund, a seasoned stock trader said, "Being able to day trade for a living successfully means reaching a level of excellence that most people will never achieve, no matter what career they choose. It's the difference between being a movie extra and an Oscar-winning actor." To earn a living in swing trading, you have to go above average. You must be willing to go the extra mile to be excellent at what you do to be successful in the trade.

Setting Goals, Objectives & Strategies for Trading

It is possible to survive and thrive in swing trading. There are many people who are doing it and you can do too. You should know that successful traders are not smarter than you, they might only be more committed and dedicated than you. If you can give your swing trading the same dedication and commitment, you will find your trading account souring with a high amount of profits.

Brain Tracy said, " Success is goals, all else is commentary." To be successful in swing trading, you need to set your yearly, quarterly, monthly and weekly trading goals. Those goals must be translated into plans and strategies which will be executed to achieve the intended results.

Execution and evaluation are very important because you can plan all you can but the only thing that counts is your ability to execute on your goals and achieve the desired outcome. Use the following steps to start setting goals and planning strategies for an effective swing trading:

1. Clarify Your Goals

It all starts with being clear about your goals. Some people claim they have goals, yet their goals are not clear enough for them to achieve them. You need to make sure you have clear goals and objectives trading. How do you start clear goals? Make them specific, measurable, attainable, realistic and time-bound (SMART). For example, " I grow my entire portfolio by 20% in six months." This goal is clear, concise and succinct. It can set you on the path of success.

2. Clarify Your Motivations

Even the best goals fail for lack of motivation. Motivation is the fire that drives you to work tirelessly in pursuance of your goals. Therefore, you need to make sure you have determined and clarified the goals you want to set for your trading activities.

Why do you want to achieve want? What will make you keep going even when the odds are set forth against you?

3. Determine Your Time Commitment

Your goals are not going to achieve themselves. You have to invest the time, energy and resources to work hard towards their achievement. Therefore, determine your time commitment per day, week and month for your trade. Make sure you are investing the right amount of time to analyze, study and evaluate and execute your trading strategy to do well in the trade.

4. Determine Your Knowledge Requirement

You need knowledge if you are going to do well in swing trading. You need to be a committed learner. You have to be continuously learning about the market and using various means to get smarter in the game. The more you learn and acquire experience in swing trading, the clearer your vision becomes and the lower your risk.

5. Determine Your Risk /Reward Ratio

What is your predetermined risk/ratio? How much money do you want to risk in every trade to achieve your trading income goal? Ideally, you might set a trading goal of 1: 3, but that will be dependent on your risk assessment and risk management ability. Know the amount of risk you want to entertain in your trading and projected reward to obtain from it.

6. Determine Your Trading Strategy

A trading strategy is a way to initiate and execute a trade to achieve your profit goals. What kind of approach do you want to use? A bearish trading strategy or a bullish trading strategy? Understand the various trading strategies and then start using one. Once you find something that is working for you, stick to the plana and use that formula to earn a lot of swing trading income.

Defining and Building a Trading Routine

You have your goals, plans, and strategies all set. What's the next thing? Your trading routine. The trading routine is the day to day activities and time commitments that will be required in working to achieve your trading/portfolio goals for each month and year. Once you define and build a trading routine, be sure to stay focused and work on it to reach your goal.

Pre-Market Hours: This is the first part of your trading time. Before the financial market opens, what do you want to start doing? What do you want to start engaging yourself with before the market opens? Well, the best thing to do with your pre-market hours is to plan, prepare for the trading day.

Consider using the news media to look at current holdings, sector, and overall market sentiments. You should also create a watchlist for opportunities and trades in the day. CNBC, Market

Watch and the other trade journals are good for your pre-market hours.

During-Market Hours: What do you need to do during market hours? You have to stay alert and vigilant. Don't get into the game of trading because everyone is doing so. As Charlie Munger said, " The money is not made in buying and selling, but waiting." Market hours are the time to enter and exit trades, but only places trades after you have waited, studied and carefully analyze a particular stock or financial instrument.

Post-Market Hours: When the market is over, you want to evaluate and measure your progress. Every day is a day for you to work towards the achievement of your trading goals and plans. Once the market is over, take the time and review what happened in the day. This can take you a couple of minutes or hours, depending on what you want to evaluate. Look at the financial market at the close of the day, monitor fluctuations and various trade indicators. Keep your eye on looking for the next upcoming swing.

Chapter Five: How to Trade

"Swing trading is a type of trading style that focuses on profiting off changing trends in price action over relatively short timeframes. Swing traders will try to capture upswings and downswings in stock prices."
~ CMC Markets

Hooray! You've decided to get into the game. To start swing trading for a living. You have probably steady aside a huge amount of savings to help you through the day to day challenges of trading life. I'm sure that you have probably learned something about swing trade, open a trading account and got some amount of money in trading capital.

What you need to do is to make sure you have you understand the basics of swing trading and how the money is made. It the end of the day, what counts is not the number of trades you've made but the average amount of growth of your portfolio over a period of time. Thus, as you set your sight on swing trading, ensure you know the fundamentals of how to earn a decent income in the game.

There are many people who simply flop when it comes to swing trading. They have this get-rich-quick idea and then starts trading with a lottery mindset. What they want to do is to just hit a one time big and then take a vacation. That's not how the game is played by successful swing traders. If you want to be excellent in the trade, you need to have a long term perspective and learn the how-to techniques to be successful in the trade.

Swing Trading as a Source of Income

The game of swing trading is all about making short term profits over a long period of time which culminates in an increase of portfolio value. You should aim at a 10% to 25% increase in your portfolio over a period of one year. There is a learning curve in swing trading, and you must also make sure you commit yourself to the learning process of earning income.

Before you get started with swing trading, you need to look at the incredible earning potential of this game. By the way, swing trading is a game; you get to lose or win at times. It is all dependent on your preparedness and effective analysis of each and every trade. This makes you have a winning edge over other traders in the market.

If you have a job, your boss will pay you every time you work. You will be paid only when you work. That means selling time for money. Swing trading is a bit different from the trading earned income stream of selling time for money. The money you earn through swing trading is known as portfolio income or paper income. This is income purely generated through carefully executed plans based on calculated risks of trading metrics and trends.

You can even earn residual income as a stock investor or trader, based on your trading plan. Many successful traders use trading and investment simultaneously to grow their portfolio. They do not spend the profits they make from trading, rather they invest in their long term investment to compound over time, where they can earn income without actively working for it. Some traders even become financially independent by learning how to trade, generate profits and invest long term to compound their earnings.

Swing Trading Rules for Making Money

If you want to make money in swing trading, you have to make sure you have set rules and regulations for trading. You can't just be like everyone else. You need to distinguish yourself by being a professional swing trader. Choose your swing trading style (short term or long term) and then make sure you have set rules to guide you in executing your trades.

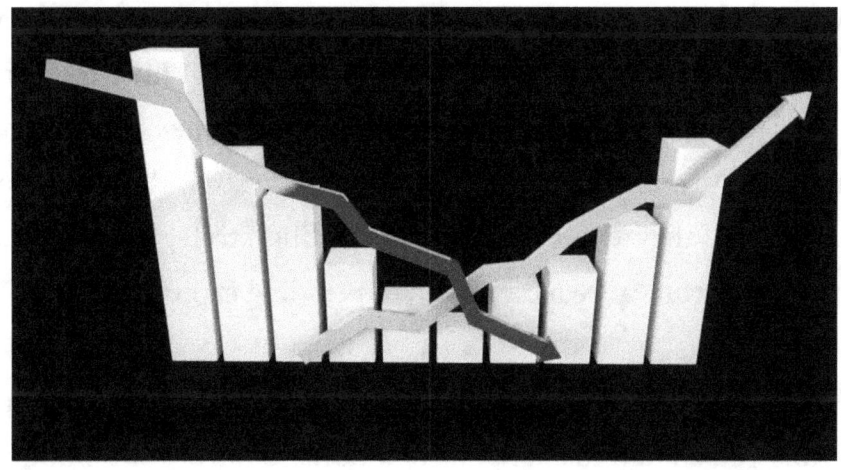

1. Always have a clear trading plan before placing a trade

There are many people who have this whole idea of buying on impulse. They have cultivated and developed this buying habit for a very long time. The problem is that they transfer their impulse buying behavior to swing trading and this causes a lot of problem for them.

You can't be successful with swing trading with an impulse buying mentality. You need to keep a close eye on the market, watch a groud of stock consistently until you develop a good instinct about new price movements. This is when buying decisions should be made. Set up a stop-loss order, establish a clear target and limit for each trade and carefully analyze a trade before committing funds to it.

2. Learn to control your emotions

When it comes to swing trading, fear and greed are the top emotions that run the actions of many traders. When they are fearful of market conditions, they execute a bearish trading strategy. At another time when they are greedy about market conditions, they execute a bullish trading strategy. Following the masses can cause a bit hit to your trading capital.

You have to preserve your trading capital from losses. That means you should master your emotions. Control your emotion of greed and fear by taking a deeper look at securities before trading. Always make sure you use a combination of technical indicators to look at whether a financial instrument is a viable trading opportunity or not. Stay objective and do your fundamental and technical analysis before trading. Evaluate your trades and learn from your experiences.

3. Always follow a group of stocks closely for a period of time

You have to keep an eye on multiple numbers of stocks daily to be able to spot an entry point for a trade. The best time for this pre-market hours. Before the marketing opens, you can decide to look at the financial news, charts, earnings reports, stock price movements, and all others.

Reading articles from trusted websites is also very important to keep a close eye on the market. Always make sure you are tracking a group of stocks at the time to launch a trade. Check highly volatile and highly traded stocks. Look for trends and volumes for trading.

4. Use multiple technical Indicators

When it comes to technical analysis, many traders simply rely on one technical analysis to forecast stock price movements. But that is not the best practice of the trade. Endeavor to use multiple technical indicators such as to find entry and exit points such as double buttons, moving average crossovers, flags and pattern tracking to find entry and exit points before placing a trade.

5. Don't rush into a trade, be patient

The problem of some people is analysis paralysis. They over-analyze and fail to take action at the eright right entry points to make wins. For some others, it simply sheer rushing into a trade because of their quest to make profits. You need a perfect balance between two. You have to know when to wait, enter and exit a trade.

Again Charlie Munger's quote says it all, " The big money is not made in the buying and selling, but in the waiting." You have to learn to wait patiently to see clear indicators of a financial instrument before moving to trade. Because some people call themselves day traders, they think they need to be placing a trade every day. Exercise patience, watch the market, invest time to due diligence before trading.

6. Always Trade With Money You Can Afford to Lose

After you have done your analysis, determined your risk/reward ratio and found the best entry points for your swing trading, one thing always comes to mind. What's that? The cash. Before you use your risk capital in any trade, ask yourself if you can afford to lose that money if the trade goes against you. Avoid being overconfident about the market.

Sometimes, the market crashes against us the most when we are too overconfident. Analyze the trade and check if you can afford to lose the money you are expending to place the trade. This will help you to be reserve and conservative with your trading.

Financial Instruments for Swing Trading

After all, is said and done, the last thing remains: getting into the game. You need to trade before you can experience any wins or make any profits. But just because you have to trade does not mean you should launch a trade into any market. Look at the financial instruments that you can start swing trading with. Take one at a time and learn to focus.

The seasoned swing traders always focus on one financial instrument and then becomes the best at it, before moving to something else. If you are looking at some financial instruments to start your swing trading, check the following: stocks, bonds, options, mutual funds, indexes, ETS, currencies, cryptos, and many others. Know your trade and focus on one financial instrument one at a time.

Chapter Six: A Deeper Look: Financial Instruments for Swing Trading

"Financial instruments are monetary contracts between parties. They can be created, traded, modified and settled. They can be cash (currency), evidence of an ownership interest in an entity (share), or a contractual right to receive or deliver cash (bond)."
~Wikepedia

When you set out to start swing trading, one of the challenging decisions to make is the kind of financial instruments to get started with. You can get overwhelmed with a host of information out there about each financial instruments and that can literally get you frustrated. It is also very important that you avoid dabbling in many financial instruments.

Jason Bond, the American stock trader said, "Call yourself a trader when your portfolio reaches $10,000. With $10,000, a swing trader can start to diversify. That means spreading out funds across picks to hedge your risk – protecting against small losses along the way. The sniper does not have this luxury." Before you reach that goal, you need to focus on one financial instrument.

Usually, when most people think about swing trading what comes to mind is stocks trading. But you need to know that swing trading is just a method of trading securities, not just stocks. You can use swing trading method to trade stocks, options, EFTs, crypto, and forex. The principles of swing trading apply across all the financial instruments, but there are pros and cons of each financial instrument.

Before you choose and select any financial instrument, you need to know how the market works and how to leverage fluctuations in pricing to make profits. Always remember that the goal in swing trading is to find a swing in the price of a financial instrument and then move in and out of the market to make a profit. If you have the right mindset and skillset, then trading any market will be a lot easy.

Swing Trading EFTs

Exchange-Traded Funds (EFTs) have become one of the best entry points for swing trading. The stock market has become very competitive and highly dominated by market players. This has paved way for many people to move unto EFT trading. Since there are over 1,400 exchange-traded funds all across the US, you can get to select various EFTs to trade.

As with every financial instrument, there are rules of the game. To succeed in trading EFTs, you have to follow simple rules of trade. One thing you have to know is that just like there are sedate and volatile stocks, there also volatile EFTs and volatile

EFTs. To increase the probability of making profits in the trade, you have to avoid sedate EFTs and then focus your attention on volatile EFTs that have a fluctuating price and high volume of trade.

Weak trends can lead to EFTs failure to yield profits during a considerable period of time. That means it is very important that you look at the charts and trends to select the best entry and exit points of EFTS before making a decision. Always make sure you have a selected number of EFTS to execute well-calculated trades o earn profits.

Look for pattern-breaking stocks that have the potential to be increasingly volatile for a period of time. A good practice for all EFT traders is to develop an EFT Swing Trading strategy. For example, you can choose to look for an upward trend and then buy EFTs that are increasing in their price as the chart moves upward. As the price moves upward to sell your EFT to pocket a decent profit.

Swing Trading Options

The beauty of swing trading options is that it can enable you to trade high priced stocks without necessary expending a lot of cash. Instead of buying the stocks at once from the stock market, you can buy an existing option of the underlying stock. To play the game of swing trading in options, it is very important to understand the fundamentals of the trade and how options work.

Options trading is simply the act of buying or selling the contract to an underlying stock sold at a strike price and set to expire at a predetermined period of time. Swing trading is a short term way of earning profit in the financial market. While you can trade options for a longer period when you are swing trading options, your goal is to find the right stock, get in and out of the game in a couple of days or weeks.

The expiration date of the option sets the tone for the swing trading. To ensure you are doing swing trading, you need to make sure you study the asset class and pick the right expiration date and strike price to earn a profit. Ideally, you have to look for "out of the money" options which are not far off, then pick a strike price that will enable the stocks to get "in the money" in a couple of weeks to earn a profit.

For those with a small amount of trading capital, options are the best place to enter the market. You can pay a premium to buy call options of high priced stocks and earn a decent profit when the market is taking an upward swing. You can also choose to buy put options of stocks that are taking a downward swing and earn money from the difference in price movements.

There are bullish and bearish trading strategies to use in options. Depending on the type of market you are dealing with, you have to make sure you are using the right strategy. Apart from the call and put options, there are other options trading techniques to use to limit your losses and maximize your gains. It is also very important that you focus your time and effort on analyzing the stock market to know the right type of stocks to select for options.

Swing Trading Stocks

For many beginner traders, you might not have the money and leveraged facility to buy many high priced stocks. But if you were to be using options, you can trade the stocks with a minimum of capital. In this case, it is advisable to go for "penny" stocks that re less than $ 10. With just $ 100 you can start swing trading stocks directly without using options.

When trading stocks, you have to define your winning strategy. You have to know that you can make thousands of dollars in cash and lose all of them in a couple of days if you fail to look at the downsides and develop a strategy for your trade.

Russek Barbour commented, *"My wife and I make extra money by trading stocks online. We started trading stocks as a side hustle when we needed to make extra money a few years ago. We had some luck early on while the market was making new highs every few months. I think everyone was making money trading at that time.*

We used our initial trading profits to pay off our student loan debt. Unfortunately, our luck did not last, and we lost $15,000 trying to trade stocks over the next 6 months. It took three years of trial and error to finally settle on a trading strategy that worked consistently for us." If you don't have a tailored trading plan that is suited for you, then you have to depend on luck to do well in the stock market.

Your goal in swing trading is to have a consistent income stream that will cover your living expenses and provide a surplus for future investments. To achieve this target, you must choose either a bullish or bearish trading strategy or both to help achieve your desired goal. You need to keep an eye on the stock price movements of you are using low cap stocks.

Swing trading favors liquid, volatile and high volume stocks that are readily available in the market. Using technical indicators you can choose to find an uptrend, then buy the underlying stock. Hold it for a while and when you see the trend continue, sell. That may mean leaving a lot of money on the table. But, it's better than the marketing crashing and losing so much money in the down market.

Swing Trading Crypto

We all know how volatile crypto currencies are. Many people have amassed fortunes in the cryptocurrency trading market. They bought cryptos at a very low priced, held it for a while and then sold it to make a huge amount of profit. But there are a lot of digital currencies in the market today, you have to decide on the ones you want to focus on.

While Bitcoins and Ethereon are the most popular ones. You can get your hands on a few cryptos as possible. Always endeavor that you stay up to date with current news and alerts about the crypto market. Things sort of change and turn very fast and you can stand the chance of getting big losses if you take your eye off the ball.

Many people bought bitcoins and held it in the e-wallet. They kept it for far too long until the value went down and then ended up losing a lot in value. The goal of swing trading is not to buy and hold for along term. You want to but an asset class, hold it for a while and when the market is favorable, sell it and then move onto the next opportunity.

The high volatility of cryptocurrencies stirs up fear and worry in many swing traders, therefore, many don't tend to swing trade cryptos. But, you don't have to worry. The same principles apply for crypto swing trading. Buy currencies at low prices, look for favorable times and then sell to make a profit and move unto the next thing.

Some brokers don't have crypto trading on their asset class. Therefore, make sure you know what the broker deals with and use a brokerage service to provide a trading opportunity for cryptocurrency swing trading opportunities. Always make sure you study the market, know the tends and the prices before placing a trade.

Swing Trading Forex

The game of forex trading is merely a game of technical analysis. As in the case of stocks where the performance operation of the underlying company can affect the stocks, their situation is different in forex trading. Therefore many forex traders use technical analysis to analyze the market and predict the new price fluctuation in international currencies.

Some of the technical analysis used in forex trading include the Elliotte Wave Theory. You have to study the trends and waves in the currency market to know where the next change is going to turn. Then you can comfortably bank your trust and plan a trade that will earn your profit. The forex market is affected by the news media, the global commodity market, and many others. Therefore, it is also very important to keep an eye of the forex market in order to get prepared to make a sale.

Chapter Seven: Tools for Trend Prediction

"To succeed with swing trading, you need to know how to read market indicators. Make a swing trade that's more likely to yield good results by getting to know the following signs of favorable conditions."
~ Omar Bassal, CFA

If you want to be successful in swing trading, you need to respect ad value trends. If you learn how to analyze, follow and predict trends, you will have a high success rate with swing trading. Many new traders simply trade on impulse and wonder why they keep losing in the market.

They have no clear strategy to analyze buying and selling signals and then how to play with the tides to make sure that they survive and thrive. But, you can't follow this way of trading if you want to stay in the game and keep on winning. You have to develop a simple, systematic and mathematical approach to trading which yields consistent results.

Oooh, yaa! You might not win in every trade. You might make mistakes in some trades at times. But here is the bottom line: when you learn how to study and use trends for swing trading, you will increase your chasing of being right and earning profits to compound your portfolio. The trend is your best friend if you are looking to make big money in swing trading.

Generally, there are two ways traders analyze and predict the prices of financial instruments: the use of industry news and chart analysis. Industry news forms a part of fundamental analysis use to determine buying and selling points in swing trading. For example, many traders tend to get afraid and begin to sell their stocks if the underlying company gets a huge lawsuit, bankrupt or experiences a series of business catastrophes.

But, you don't have to depend on the fundamental news from the media. You can also use price chart analysis to predict the price movements of financial instruments. Once, you start using price charts, you will understand the need to find trends and learn how to predict trends so that you can be in the position to make better buying and selling decisions.

In a nutshell, swing trading is all about buying financial instruments at a low price and selling them high to make a profit. The challenge is knowing what to buy when to buy and then when to sell. If you buy the right stocks and sold them at the right time, you will make a profit and do well in your swing trading. But, the question is: how do you know when to buy (entry point) and when to sell (exit point)? This is where trend analysis and predictions come in.

Trend & Wave Analysis

When you want to talk about waves and trend prediction in the financial market, you can't forget about a man named Ralph Nelson Elliotte. Through his discovery and analysis of the stock market in the early nineteenth century, many people have realized that stock price movements are not something magical, mystical and unpredictable.

According to Elliott Wave Theory, " The financial market trades in repetitive market cycles, rather than unrepetitive manner." Elliott realized that the everyday condition of the financial market is highly influenced by the "predominant action of the masses and investor reaction to outside forces." He noticed that the way many brokers and traders react to the stock market affects the upward and downward movement in the prices of stocks.

That means if you can understand the pattern in human behavior and use those indicators very well, you can see the trends to buy, sell or wait in the financial market. In Elliott discovery, he was known for his consistent use of fractal nature, which refers to the unending repetitive nature of price action and market reactions.

In simple terms, when the price of a stock goes high, many people will start selling. And then when the price of the stock begins to go down, many traders will start buying. This is a simple buying and selling pattern of trade participants in the financial market. According to the Dow Theory also, " the price of stocks moves in waves."

Hence, a firm foundation in technical analysis can enable you to do well analyzing patterns in stock price movements. Elliott's Wave Theory reveals that there are five main patterns in the movement of financial instruments: " In an upward trend, a five-way rise will be followed by a three-way fall; in a downward trend, a five-way fall will be followed by a three-way rise. Finally, the prices of financial instruments decline on wave four due to price booking."

If you noticed the theory, you'll notice that it helps you to predict the future direction of the market as well as whether a certain financial instrument will rise and fall, based on current market conditions. That means you can use the trends and waves to know when to initiate a stop loss and which types of the market to place a trade as well as entry points.

Please, take note that even though this theory has been accepted globally due to their positive result, you should be using more than two indicators and pattern analyzing to finalize your trade decisions. Avoid making trade decisions on just a simple indicator or pattern prediction.

Trend Lines and Trend Prediction

Once you understand trends and how they work, the next step is to start using trend lines for stock price predictions. Trend lines help you to find the exact entry points to buy a particular stock, option, EFT or commodity. It also shows you the exact exit point to begin to sell the underlying security so that you can realize a profit from the trade transaction.

Entry and exit points are gold in swing trading. You want to know when to enter an when to exit the market so that you can earn profits. Choosing entry points can mean making a win or loss in swing trading. In some cases, your prediction on the direction of the market might be right, but the problem might be selecting the entry and exit points.

By plotting and drawing trend lines, you can be able to find when to enter and exit a market. First, you need to know that trend lines are slopping lines on price charts of financial instruments while stop and resistance are the horizontal lines. Both lines help to detect buying and selling signals, but you have to know how to use each one appropriately.

Convergence is when trend lines meet with indicators, establishing buying and selling signals to start initiating trading decisions for particular financial instruments. To draw a trend line, select two swing points of a particular stock (for example) and then connect the points so that they touch each other. You'll notice that you'll have a steep slope on the chart price.

EMC Corp. (EMC) NYSE   © StockCharts.com
11-Feb-2000 4:00pm Open 54.50 High 59.88 Low 53.59 Last 57.12 Volume 51.5M Chg +2.12 ▲
W EMC 57.12 (Weekly)

If the trend gets steeper, you have to know that it indicates that the market trend is getting stronger, possibly showing buying urge in trade participants. You can also check if the trend line is breaking out. You can plot trend lines at stockcharts.com. A breaking trend line helps you to time the market to buy at the appropriate time and make a hit. The best strategy is to combine both support and resistance lines to make a better trading decision.

How to Follow the Trend

Swing trading is a game of trend following. If you understand trend indicators and follow them appropriately, you'll find yourself making the right trading decisions that will lead to consistent profits over a period of time. Following trends is not rocket science, but it takes time and practice to get used to both resistance and support lines to make good trade decisions.

What you need to remember is that the trend line between two points must show the need to enter and exit a trade. The trend line must also be "wide enough to capture a trade", as the experts will say. The wider the trend line, the higher your possibility of making more profits from the single trade transaction. Using your trading strategy, you should be able to initiate a trade based on the trend line analysis.

Let's use stocks trading as an example.
On the stock charts, there are various stocks to select and analyze. If you are using a bullish trading strategy, then you have to look for stocks that are experiencing an increase in the share price. As long as the share price goes higher and higher, the stock will be in an uptrend and the stock chart will show a direction of stock prices going upward.

This is just but the beginning. The key is to look for stocks experiencing a strong trend. After you notice a strong uptrend in the underlying stock, wait for the perfect time to buy the stock. The assumption here is that the market will still be moving upward which will increase the value of the stock you bought at an earlier date.

Support & Resistance Trigger Graph

Plot support and resistance lines for the stock that is experiencing an upward trend. Using support and resistance lines, begin to find buying selling signals for the stock. Keep watch over the support lines: when the price of the stock falls to the support line, it is an indication that many trade participants will buy at the current stock price. This has a way of causing the price of the stock to fall back again.

But when the price of a stock increases to the resistance level, it signifies an indication that other traders in the market will sell the stock they already own. If you buy a stock on an uptrend and then wait for the resistance level indicator to sell, you will end up making losses. These are just higher probabilities. Therefore, you should stay calm about the market and don't be overconfident because of prevailing technical indicators.

What's The Best Swing Trading Indicator For You?

There are various technical indicators to use for a trade. You have to learn a few of them and then master them. Don't be confused by the cacophony of noises in the stock market about these technical indicators. Find a couple of them and then practice using them to find entry and exit points to make a trade. When you find success using them, stick to them.

Austin Drysdale, a seasoned swing trader said, *"If you are a new trader then it is very important for you to understand that no indicator or oscillator is going to make your trade profitably immediately, so don't go on a wild goose chase to find one that will. Learn a select few indicators and the methods and strategies to use them effectively. Master them, and then learn more. Your strategy will be more profitable using fewer indicators that you have mastered. Then more indicators that you haven't."*

That is the key. Don't get confused by many indicators for analyzing financial instruments. Select a few of them and become an expert at using them. Popular technical indicators used by many people in swing trading include the following: support and resistance levels, 10 and 20-day simple moving averages, (SMA), channel trading, Fibonacci retracement, and MACD crossovers. Find what works for the trading plan and then stick the methods and strategies of using them.

Chapter Eight: Fundamental Analysis Explained

"Fundamental analysis is a method of measuring a security's intrinsic value by examining related economic and financial factors."

~Investopedia

Whether you are trading or investing, you need to have a good understanding of fundamental analysis for evaluating a stock or any other financial instrument. While swing traders can depend on technical analysis, it pays to do your technical analysis and then finally back it up with fundamental analysis. Combining technical and fundamental analysis help to buttress your point and reduce your risk of making mistakes.

Many traders seem to avoid fundamental analysis in their trading activities. They think it is complicated and has nothing to do with their trading activities. Well, that is far from the trust. The fact is fundamental analysis plays a big role in analyzing a stock if you are planning to invest or trade.

This is also very important in understanding fundamental analysis: many traders seek to find the variation in stock prices so that they can earn profits from the sale of the underlying stock. In this regard, they are not seeking to find the intrinsic value of a stock and then compare with the share price to know whether it is underpriced and overpriced.

Investors invest for the long term. They aim at buying undervalued stocks and then holding them for a long time to compound their dividend earnings and the value of the stock as well. Typically, investors can hold a stock for one to twenty years and then collect dividends. They are not looking at selling the stock to make a profit. What they want is a steady annual dividend which would be compounded over a period of time they are holding the stock.

What is Fundamental Analysis?

Fundamental analysis is the main method used by investors to find the value of a stock and know whether to invest or not. A fundamental investor can sometimes be a business owner looking to buy other businesses to add to their portfolio. In this regard, they have to look at the financial statements of the company, industry and performance reports as well as other business information to know whether the company is worth buying or not.

Investors want to know the annual revenue of the company. They want to know the debt to equity ratio of the company. They are looking to know gross profit, net operating profit, and return on shareholder's equity for a period of time. These are the key information required by investors to make good investment decisions. And you know, this information cannot be found by reading stock price charts and following the stock market predictions.

This information can be obtained by reading the annual reports of companies, industry news and finding the competition of the company. This is the reason many investors tend to be aloof when it comes to checking and getting information from the stock market. They are so much focused on the fundamental facts surrounding the company to the extent that they pay less attention to the price fluctuation and the volatility of the stock.

Fundamental analysis is defined as the process of finding or measuring the intrinsic value of a stock. To achieve these results, investors look for a company's revenue, expenses, assets, liabilities, and earnings potential to know whether the company is worth investing or not. Through annual reports and industry-related reports, the value of a stock is determined and compared against the share price of the stock in the financial market.

Indicators for Fundamental Analysis

Just like technical analysis has indicators, the fundamental analysis also has indicators. Investors try to use these indicators to make stock buying and selling decisions. They also use the indicators to know when to enter and exit the market. The basic idea behind fundamental analysis is the fact that the share value of a company is influenced by the health of the underlying company.

In some cases, this can be true. But if you look at other factors, you'll notice that there are other outside factors that determine the share value of a stock. The supply and demand forces of the market also tend to affect the liquidity, volume, and volatility of stocks. In the meantime, the following is a list of factors used by fundamental analyst use to determine the value of a stock.

1. Revenue

Investors want to look at a company with rising revenues. A rising revenue is an indicator that a couple is no path of growth. Revenue reports are reported on an annual and quarterly basis. At the end of each business quarter, publicly traded companies provide a quarterly projection of their revenues, expenses, and profits. And then these reports are being validated and checked with the actual projections made.

Company revenues can be affected by a myriad of factors: a seasonal rise in demand, competitor actions and holiday seasons. When a company outperforms its sales and revenue projections, it baffles active traders and investors, leading to a high demand for the company's stock. Demand forces tend to increase the price of the stock and causes an upward trend to be set forth in the motion.

2. Earnings Per Share

At the end of the day, what investors want is higher earnings per share. In some cases, a company can be experiencing growth and then find that their operating expenses are eating up their revenue. Companies of these type make a high amount of revenues, but due to high operating and management expenses, they tend to delivery low earnings per share to shareholders.

What investors do is to look for companies in the same sector and they analyze their earnings per share to who is doing better than the other. Generally, companies with higher profit margins have higher earnings per share. Ability to pay off dividends to shareholders is also very important. An announcement that a company is going to be paying dividends can also increase the demand for the stocks and thus increasing the value of the share price.

3. P/E Ratio

P/E Ratio is known as the price per earnings of a stock. It helps to know the valuation of a stock: as to whether a stock is undervalued or overvalued. Stocks are sold at X number of their earning potential. For example, if ABC company is currently trading at $ 240 per share and has earned $ 24 per share during a period of one year, the P/E ratio can be said to be 10. That means the company is trading $ 10 times their earning potential.

4. Business & Sector News

This is a very important factor in determining the value of a stock. Important news like downsizing, bankruptcy, lawsuits of low sector performance affects the psychological behavior of traders leading to buying and selling actions in the market. An upswing in the value of a stock can be influenced by the fundamental news of a company releases into the public domain. You have to keep an eye on the sector and industry news reports to be able to analyze the reaction of the market.

To do well in swing trading, you have to use technical analysis and then back it up with the fundamental valuation. All it takes is practice and repetition for a period of time. The more you use fundamental analysis to evaluate and analyze the market behavior of a stock, the faster you will get to understand how everything really works and take advantage of opportunities.

Chapter Nine: Technical Analysis

"The better you become at technical analysis, the more efficient and profitable your swing trades will be."
~ Melvin Pasternak

It all starts with getting your skills right. In every business, there are skills to be learned and acquired. The skills make ou efficient and effective in running operations. In the business world, a microprenueur needs business skills such as marketing, sales, administration, cash flow management, and many others. The more skillful the business owner, the higher the propensity of becoming successful.

Swing trading is no different. To be a successful swing trader, you need to focus on developing the skills of analyzing trades, markets, and securities. The better you are at analyzing markets and traders, the more profitable will be at swing trading. You will find yourself avoiding deadly mistakes that kill many beginner swing traders.

As a matter of fact, you need skills or you'll be skilled in swing trading. One of the most important skills that are essential for swing trading is technical analysis. The fact is that you can't be a successful swing trader without learning the basics and advanced strategies used in technical analysis. Analyzing a trade before entering reduces your risk and increases your earning potential.

Melvin Pasternak, a leading swing trader says it all when made the statement: *"The better you become at technical analysis, the more efficient and profitable your swing trades will be."* With that said, what you want to do is to start learning the basics of technical analysis, putting your knowledge into practice and then evaluating your predictions and wins as you become more skillful in technical analysis.

What is technical analysis?

Well, technical analysis is the process of attempting to predict the future prices of financial instruments using indicators, charts, and trends. By looking at price charts and various theories, the price of a financial instrument can be predicted. Upon this prediction, trades can be made. The securities under consideration can include stocks, mutual funds, index funds, currencies, commodities, and many others.

While fundamental analysis deals with analyzing a stock from the inside, technical analysis deals with analyzing a company from the outside. A technical analyst does not need to read the financial reports of a company to be able to predict immediate stock prices. Through stock charts and listening to the latest news about the company, the stock prices can be predicted with accuracy for profitable swing trading.

Stock Charts

If you're going to learn technical analysis, then the very first place to start is reading stock charts. Not being able to read stock charts is like investing blindly and hoping things work well. A stock chart is much more like an X-Ray, giving you insight into how the stock market is performing, which stocks are taking a downward trend and which are taking an upward trend. Reading a stock chart enables you to know what is happening in the stock market so that you can be prepared to take action.

Each publicly-traded company has a stock chart. This stock chart outlines and provides details of how the stock is performing, what is going on and any other basic information about the underlying company. The stock chart comes in the form of a graph, showing the direction of the stock growth or value in terms of price fluctuations over a period of time.

Each stock chart provides specific information on the underlying company's stock: current trading price, dividends, trading volume, historical highs or lows, and price fluctuations over a period of time and others. To the fundamental analyst, the stock is a reflection of the happening in the company. If the company does well, its stock will also do well by growing and increasing in value.

There are several stock charts: bar charts, line charts, and candlestick charts. The same item is on all these three stock charts. But the main difference is how each stock is represented. Understanding how these three stock charts work and operate is key in reading them.

Line & Bar Charts

The line chart uses the last stock price to track price movements while the bar charts make use of the lowest and highest stock price as well as the closing price to tell the performance of the underlying stock of a company.

Candlestick Charts

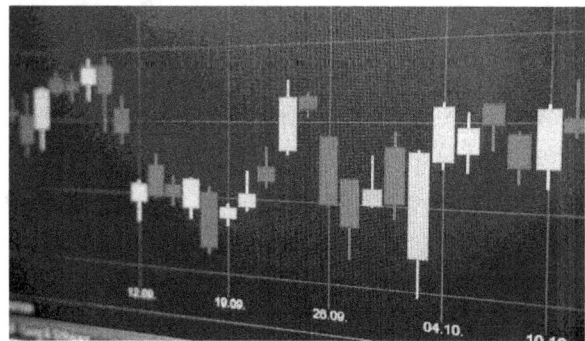

Candlestick charts show open, closing, high and low prices of a security within a period of time. The candle stock charts help investors and traders to detect buying and selling signals for initiating a trade. The black/red color indicates whether a stock traded lower than its opening price while the black/red colors show whether a stock traded higher than its opening price.

A key item to look for on a candlestick chart is to find where the buying pressure is. The buying pressure of a stock indicates the presence of a bullish market. This can be observed and seen on the long white/green candlesticks on the stock chart. The opening and closing prices on the candlestick helps to determine whether the market is experiencing a downward movement or an upward movement. This helps to know the exit and entry point based on your trading plan.

Key Items On Stock Chart

There are a couple of things on every stock chart. To be able to predict and understand stock charts, you need to know what those things mean and what they stand for. The following are the key items you should know to be able to read stock charts:

1. Ticker Symbol: This is a trade symbol used to represent and differentiate one publicly traded stock from one another. It is found on the ticker column. For example, Apple stocks are designated with AAPL while Microsoft stocks have been designated with MSFT.

2. The 52-Week High And Low: It reveals the highest and lowest prices for which a specific stock of a company traded within a one year period. It helps to predict the future performance of a stock. The volatility of a stock can be predicated on this.

3. P/E Ratio: This is a very important yardstick for measuring and evaluating stocks. The price per earnings (P/E) can be obtained by dividing the current trading price of the stock over the earnings per share.

4. Dividend/Per Share: This refers to the annual payments of investor's return on investments. Some companies focus on using the earnings to promote and contribute to further growth of the company while others make annual payments of the dividends. The amount of dividend paid is represented on the stock chart.

5. Dividend Yield: The dividend yield seeks to tell investors the growth of their investments with the underlying company. It is founded by dividing the current dividend by the current stock price.

6. Open Price: This is the price at which the stock has open for each trading day.

7. Close Price: This is price at which the stock closes when trading day is over.

8. Previous Close: The previous close is the price at which the stock closed a day before. It helps to know whether a stock is moving up or down.

9. Net Close: This the variation in the closing prices of the previous day and the current trading day. The net close helps to know when the stock price is moving upward or downward.

10. Day High, Day Low: This shows the peak and valley prices for which a stock traded during the day. This is very important for day traders since it helps them to make gains and profits through the day high and day low values.

Reading the Stock Chart: Key Things to Know

As long as you understand the key items that make up a stock chart, the next step you want to take is to begin to read the stock chart. Reading a stock chart is not hard at all.

The following are the key things to know and do when reading a stock chart:

1. Look for the price and time axes.

The price and time axes are the two most important areas of a stock chart. This is where it all starts. The vertical axis points to the prices of the stock over a period of time. There are several prices ranges on the stock, clarifying the movement of the price of the stock over a period of time. The horizontal axis points to the time for which price changes take place on the chart.

2. Look for the trend lines

Once you have a close look at the price and time axes and have seen the movement in the price of a stock over a period of time, you want to look at the trend line. The trend line tells you the price of a stock over a period of time. The trend line is not obvious on the price chart; you have to plot the trend line by joining two prices/time on the stock chart.

3. Look for the trading volume

The trading volume of the stock is always shown at the bottom of the stock chart in green and red bars. It can sometimes be blue or purple bars. An increase in the trading volume of a stock indicates the strength of a trend over a period of time. Check the strength of the stock, either for a downward trend line or an upward trend line.

4. Look for support and resistance lines

The support and resistance lines are one of the most important things to look for in a stock chart since they help predict buying and selling signals. The support line is the price at which a stock trading upward cannot pass by while the resistance line is the price at which a stock trading downward cannot pass by. The resistance line keeps the stock's price from moving up any further and vice versa. They are horizontal lines plotted on the stock chart along with the trend line.

Important Technical Indicators

It is one thing to read a stock chart and another thing to understand them. If you read the technical indicator but could not understand than your chances of doing very well in analyzing a stock will be curtailed. What you want to do is to read the stock and then use the knowledge of technical indicators tell what the stock chart is saying and predicting in the future.

Support & Resistance Lines

What do they mean? They tell you where selling and buying pressure of the market is really strong. Knowing this indicator helps to enter a trade at the bounce of the support line. In order words, swing traders are looking to buy stocks at stock and then sell at resistance lines. Stop-loss is placed below the support line.

The resistance lines tell you of the price area where selling pressure is so high to the extent that it outwits the buying pressure of the market. At this stage, the price of the underlying stock hits and bounce back against an upward trend. Stop-loss orders are placed above the resistance line.

Another key thing to know is that when support and resistance lines breach, they swing roles and the cycle begins again. You can use the knowledge of support and resistance to make better buying and selling decisions which will yield better results over time.

Simple Moving Averages (SMA)

This technical indicator is used to calculate the average price of a stock over a period of time. For example, a 10 Day SMA is used to find the average new price of a stock by calculating the closing price of a stock for 10 trading days and then dividing it by 10. For a 20 Day SMA the average new price will be calculated by diving the closing prices of stock in 20 days by 20.

These two SMAs can be used to determine buying signals in the market. For example, when the SMA (10) crosses the SMA (20), it will mean that an impending upward trend is looming in the market which will be creating a buying pressure. The reverse is a way to predict a downward trend, which will create selling pressure in the market.

MACD Crossover

The MACD is composed of two main lines: MACD and the signal line. The reaction between these two lines determines whether to buy and to sell a stock or any security in the market. For example, when the MACD crosses above the signal line, it tells that there is going to be a bullish market that will mean a time to start buying stocks.

On the other hand, when the MACD line crosses below the signal line, it will mean that a bear market is about to set in and thus a swing trader needs to get ready to buy. The discipline is to wait for these lines to cross each other before making buying and selling decisions. Again, you have to wait for the lines to cross again to enter a trend reversal trade. Entry points give you signals to start buying while exit points give you the signal to start buying a stock.

Chapter Ten: Strategies to Apply Immediately

"Stock picking is hard, and understanding stock charts is the first step toward success."
~ Chris Muller

Whether you are trading stocks, options, forex or currencies, one thing still exists: you want to earn huge profits in a short period of time. To achieve this result you need to use the right trade strategies to catch profits and avoid a losing position in the market. If you buy low and sell high, you will make profits. That is the punch line.

In every market, there are two main trends: an uptrend and downtrend. To take advantage of trend lines to do very well trading, then you need to master the pullback trading strategy. Experience and results have shown that trend trading and the pullback strategy is the most profitable method to reap profits from swing trading and be a success.

1. "Catch the Trend" Strategy

So, we want to take a look of this all amazing "catch the trend" trading strategy and how to use is it to generate profits in the market. The usual buy low and sell high is actually a pullback trading strategy. You buy a security at a lower price when the trend begins and then you sell high when the trend reaches its peak. This is why they say, " Trend is your friend." You have to keep watch of the trend lines as you wait for the trend to reach its peak to reap high profits.

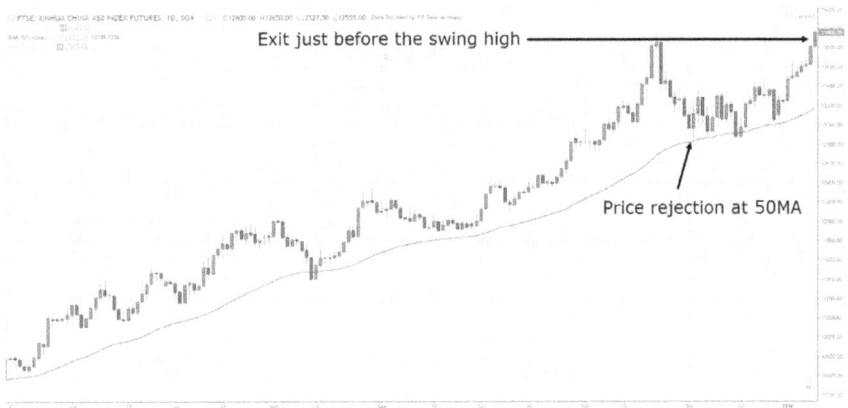

A pullback strategy means that you are trading in the direction of a prevailing trend. You're trying to assume that the trend has just started and then follow the trend to buy financial instruments and then sell them. To use the pullback strategy, you need to be familiar with Fibonacci Retracement Indicator and the Support & Resistance Triggers. You can closely use this strategy in the currency market when you notice that a particular currency is taking on a particular trend for a period of time.

2. " Go Against the Trend" Strategy

Notice that is the first strategy, you are looking for a trend movement and then follow the trend to buy and sell financial instruments. In this case, you completely go against the trend. It is also known as "counter-trend" because you trying to predict the price movement of commodities against the momentum of a trend.

How does this strategy work? Find a strong momentum that equates to the previous price height of resistance, and then look for where the price rejection begins to emerge. You can detect this by analyzing and identifying the trend as the candle forms a strong bearish close in the market. Once these key indicators have emerged, buy on the next candle and then try to set your stop loss at 1 ATR above the highs. If everything goes well, your wing trade will go through and you'll reap profits. But you have to make sure you take profits swing goes low again. You can use this strategy in the forex

3. "Range Market" Strategy

In this strategy, what you are trying to do is to study the stock charts and find where the price of financial instruments have gotten stock in particular market range. Once you find this indicator, you can organize your buying and selling within this geographical region. To use this strategy, you need to know-how support and resistance trigger really work.

This strategy is usually used in stock swing trading. You identify where the price breaks below Support and then wait for a strong price rejection to buy at the next candle open. Before the next resistance, you have to take your profits and then set your stop loss 1 ATR below the candle low.

4. "Double Bottom Reversal" Strategy

The focus of this strategy is how to use double top chart patterns to execute a swing trade. This strategy is best applied by looking at a market whose bearish trend is coming to a close.

It is simply a bullish reversal strategy where a bearish trend at support retraces until it gets to the resistance level again.

Source: Trading Strategy Guide

When this happens, it is an indication that most traders will be ready to sell. Here are the three things to keep in mind when executing this strategy: a strong bearish trend, two equal bottoms at Support and "candlestick breakout of the neckline." You should initiate a buying trade when the double bottom breakout candle closes above the neckline and then take profit at the same price distance from the highest peak of the Neckline.

5. "Double Top Pattern" Strategy

The double top pattern strategy is a bearish reversal indicator occurring just after an extended period of a bullish trend. In this strategy, the main focus is to sell the underlying security on the downtrend. This strategy can be used in forex trading to maximize gains.

Once you notice that the characteristics of a bottom-top strategy, the strategy is to wait for the breakout candle to close below the neckline in order to buy the underlying security. Your stop loss has to be placed slightly above the resistance of the double top pattern. You will then have to catch up with profits 2 or3 times away from the highest pick of the neckline.

Chapter Eleven: How to Apply the Swing Trading Strategies

"All you need is one pattern to make a living."
~ Linda Raschke.

It's one thing to know how the strategies work and another thing to use them appropriately to make profits in swing trading. When it comes to applying strategies, some of the important things to always consider is entry points, exit points, profit levels, and stop-loss levels. All the swing trading strategies are all about helping you figure these things out based on the condition of the market at the time.

Let's take a look at how we can use some of the strategies discussed in chapter nine to execute swing trading and make consistent wins in the market. Before we begin, you need to know and understand that the market is always changing and you can just be trading on one strategy.

As they say, "Practice makes perfect." You have to learn one strategy and put it practice one at a time to do well in the long term. You need to understand the strategies, notice their technical indicators and learn how to use them based on the state of the market at the time.

Pullback Strategy Example (Stocks)

Let's say that ABC stock is the underlying sock of a technology company. The stock has been doing well for a period of time. After its quarterly earnings reports, which shows up as an incredible performance, many traders know that following positive earnings reports, the share price will likely go up. Therefore, they decided to buy the stock. The following days after, the share price went as high as 20%.

Once swing traders realized that they have made huge profits, then started exiting the trade, which suddenly causes the market to contract and the price of ABC stock to "pull back." It is very important for you to know that the "pull back" of a stock is not because of any negative action. It is due to the action of many short term traders in the market.

Since the underlying company is doing well, many long term traders and investors will keep buying the stock which will increase the trend again. This is how the pullback strategy works.

"Range Market" Strategy Example (Currency/Options)

In every options trade, there is an expiration date. If you are buying call options, then you need to make sure the underlying stocks get in the money to make a profit. Time is very important is stock options because you are predicting that the stock will get ITM within a period fo time. Let's see how the "range market" strategy works for options swing trading for a currency.

Let's say XYZ stock has been trading around $ 120 per share. Suddenly, the stock price begins to move to support levels on the chart. Therefore you bought 2 contracts of call options at a premium of $ 1. 5 For two contracts, the total costs will be $ 300 (100x2x1.5). After the purchase, the trader simply waits patiently from the stock price to get to resistance levels. As this happens, the trader sells the underlying stock and pocket an amount from the variation in stock prices. It is very important to wait for the resistance and support triggers before executing any trade action.

Direction Following Options Strategies

The most common trade placed in options calls and put options. When a trader expects a bearish market, that the market will be taking on an uptrend, the trader will sell call options to collect premiums. While you sell call options to collect premiums, the downsides are when the stock goes up in value again. At this stage, you'd notice that you have left a lot of money on the table.

On the other hand, you can execute a put option on any financial instrument. To capitalize on the market, you decided to sell put options. A put option is an indicator that the market will be going down in value. For example, you have realized that the price of gold, selling at $ 1200 will be going down in value as a result of certain technical indicators and fundamental news events. If you are using options, you can just sell put options to safeguard your position against the bearish market.

In this case, you will collect the premiums from the sale of the put option. If the price of gold goes down as predicted, then you will be forced to sell your ounce of good to the next party. However, if the market didn't o down as implied, you collect the premium and still keep your gold.

If after you bought the crypto, the value still drops in value, you made a profit. But if the price of the crypto increased in value a few days after you sold your stock. You will get premiums but leave so much money on the table. Trend lines help to know when to execute the strategy to cut your losses in the trade.

Using Breakouts for Currency Trading

If you are trading in cryptos or any other currency, one of the best strategies to do well in the game is with breakouts. The breakouts strategy makes uses of support and resistance to enter and exit trades. So what happens is that the currency or coin either breaks upward above the resistance level of breaks downward above the support levels.

Once the currency starts trading at this level, the market will become volatile and you can then follow the breakout direction to knock your profits. As soon as the coin starts trading beyond that new support, volatility in the market tends to increase which means prices will generally follow through the breakout direction.

Chapter Twelve: Swing Trading Rules

"Where you want to be is always in control, never wishing, always trading, and always first and foremost protecting your butt."

– Paul Tudor Jones.

Always remember what swing trading is: a trading methodology that is used to generate profit in the short term by looking for variation in trends of financial instruments to generate profits. The aim is to capture short terms profits through technical analysis of financial instruments.

A Perfect Guide for Swing Trading

Thus, you need to learn the tricks and hacks of technical analysis and how to apply it to your swing trading. If you are looking to begin making profits in the financial market, this simple but profound guide should help you to do so:

1. Look for a group of stocks to start analyzing

Looking at the stock charts and the financial market, selecting taking a closer look at stocks or any financial instruments to start analyzing. Many stock swing traders focus their efforts on "penny stocks" with high volatility and then capitalize on their upward swing to make profits. Find the group of sector stock or financial instruments that best meets your need. You have to also know that technical analysis is your friend, to do well in swing trading, you must learn the skills of technical analysis. This skills will then be used to analyze the stock you selected and when to determine the entry and exit point for the underlying stock.

2. Leverage the Power of Trend Lines

The first technical indicator that you must get used to is trend lines. Trend lines are the most powerful technical tools to use in swing trading. Your goal here is to find stocks with an upward trend and then try to plot a slopping graph that outlines the peaks and valleys of the stock price. Once you see this signal, know that a buying pressure is going to mount on the market, causing many traders to start buying positions.

But as the pattern reverses with a downward trend, you should know that this is a signal for traders to start selling positions in order to capture profits. Drawing the trend lines will enable you to see a clearer view of market reactions and better position yourself to be a key player and winner in the financial market.

3. Buttress Your Point with Support & Resistance Triggers

Support and resistance are just other tools to detect entry and exit points in swing trading. These lines emanate from the trendline and moving averages. As you detect buying and selling signal with trend lines, draw support and resistant horizontal lines to buttress your initial technical indication of the market. If the results collide, you should know that the same thing is likely to happen.

4. Use Candlesticks to analyze Swing Trading Moves

Even though this technique is not used by many traders, expert traders know how valuable it is. Candlesticks work almost like stock charts to help you detect the best entry and exit points for a particular trade. You find where stock price movements swing upward and downward and then when to place a trade to take over a certain amount of profit in the marketplace. It helps to ensure that your trades are safe and sound.

5. Look at the Fundamental News Behind the Analysis

You can use technical analysis to find when to buy and sell and make the right trading decisions. But looking for the underlying fundamental news that triggers a movement in stock price helps to limit your losses and increase your gains. If you're predicting an upward trend in stock prices, what might the fundamental trigger responsible for that change?

Could it be the company has announced a stock split which has triggered buying behavior in the market place and possibly decreases in the price of stocks? What could the news be? Search that out. Finding the fundamental news and matching it with the technical indicators from the tools will give you confidence level and increase your rate of winning in the swing trading.

How to Develop A Profitable Trading System?

If you're going to excel at swing trading, then you need a profitable trading system. What is a profitable trading system? It is a system, pattern or way of trading that generates consistent profits. The test of your trading system is your ability to generate consistent profits in your trading accounts over time. That's the key.

If you are swing trading from home or your home office, one the things you will realize is that there will be no one there with you to motivate, educate and encourage you. The success or failure of your swing trading is highly dependent on your ability to develop the right habits, attitudes, and skillset to make you successful through an upmarket and a down market.

To do well in swing trading, you need to be focused on generating consistent profits over a period of time. That's what counts. Your focus should be directed and concentrated on consistent profits. Because at the end of the day, that's what really counts. Sometimes, you may lose in a trade, but at the end of it all, you want to make sure you have way more profits than losses. That is what consistent profits mean.

Analyze your results. Are you getting consistent profits or consistent losses? If you already experiencing consistent losses, it is a revelation that your trading system is weak and in a problem. To reverse the equation and make sure your trading system turns in consistent profits, you need to review your trading pattern, behavior and way of life. Which part of your trading system is weak?

Whether you are a day trader, swing trader, trend trader or what evet, you have to endeavor to develop a trading system that empowers you to be successful. Avoid taking an impulsive trading decision. Stick to the elements to your trading plan, avoid being greedy and investing all your trading capital with a hope that a particular trade will do well.

A key area to also look at is your money management and self-discipline. You need to look at swing trading as a business. If you have good management and self-discipline, it will enable to manage your profits rather than blow through frivolous activities. This is very important because people start making profits and then spending with no plan in place.

Keep a journal of all your trades. Even though your brokerage account offers you a system of managing your trade, it is a good practice to keep a journey of all your trade analysis, trade placing and wins and losses. Keeping an hour journal enables you to think on paper and review your plans and actions. This prevents you from making hasty decisions.

Celebrate your wins. This is very important to keep the momentum going. Be happy about any kind of win you have made and ensure that you keep the momentum going in your direction. Put forth the right attitude and thoughts towards your swing trading. Believe in yourself and your swing trading abilities. Have faith that you can make it swing trading and you'll surely succeed.

Know when to go off-book. While sticking to your plan, even when your emotions are telling you to ignore it, is the mark of a successful trader, this in no way means that you must blindly follow your plan 100 percent of the time. You will, without a doubt, find yourself in a situation from time to time where your plan is going to be rendered completely useless by something outside of your control. You need to be aware enough of your plan's weaknesses, as well as changing market conditions, to know when following your predetermined course of action is going to lead to failure instead of success. Knowing when the situation really is changing, versus when your emotions are trying to hold sway is something that will come with practice, but even being aware of the disparity is a huge step in the right direction.

Avoid hanging on too tightly to your starter strategy. The personalized trading strategy that you first create is an important step in trading properly, no two ways around it.

That doesn't mean that it is the last strategy that you are ever going to need, however, far from it. Your core trading strategy is one that should always be constantly evolving as the circumstances surrounding your trading habits change and evolve as well. What's more, outside of your primary strategy you are going to want to eventually create additional plans that are more specifically tailored to various market states or specific strategies that are only useful in a narrow band of situations. Remember, the more prepared you are prior to starting a day's worth of trading, the greater your overall profit level is likely to be, it is as simple as that.

Chapter Thirteen: Risk Management for Swing Trading

"A losing trader can do little to transform himself into a winning trader. A losing trader is not going to want to transform himself. That's the kind of thing winning traders do"
– Garry Bielfeldt.

The day you open your brokerage account, you will notice that you have entered a different kind of world. Whether you are investing or trading, there is an amount of risk in every trade. You have to know that the odds are against you, but what you'll do is to maximize the loss to make wins. That's the central strategy you need to have.

All too soon, many beginner traders get wiped out of the game because they fail to analyze and manage their risk. You have to understand that swing trading is a game of risk. And you are the chief risk offer of your swing trading. You must have a clear and strict standard of trading that ensures you do what is required to cut your losses and maximize your wins.

For many people, because they are using an online trading platform, they seem not to do their evaluations and analysis before making a trade. That's a big mistake. Always learn to use your journal to make prior calculations and thorough analysis before placing a trade. You need to understand that every money you invest in trading is a risk and you need to get rewarded for taking that risk.

The key to success in swing trading is to manage your risks carefully. While it is good to hear success stories. Don't let those successes get into your head. Stay objective and conservative in your trading. Always know that you can lose all your trading capital in the game of swing trading. But managing your risk and taking a critical look at each trade you place will enable you to do well in your trading activities.

Risk management is central if you're going to do well. Some people say that trading is risky. But if you take a look at it, risk comes from not understanding, analyzing and knowing what you are doing. To minimize your risk of trading, educate yourself and keep learning. The more you learn and know about swing trading, the better you minimize your risks and get a clearer look at the swing trading.

Always remember that there is no free lunch in swing trading. Every trade that you place is a risk. Therefore, only place a trade when you can afford the money you use. It is also very important that you cut your losses and make sure every swing trading strategy has been well thought off and well planned to generate the intended results. If you manage your risks very well, the end results are that you'll stay in the game for long and compound your portfolio.

Swing Trading Success – Risk Management Strategy

Nobody wants to take a losing position on trade. But it just simply happens. Knowing that each trade has a risk in it means that you'll need to need to have a risk management system to help you trade in a professional manner where you follow a specific step by step process to achieve the planned results of your swing trading.

1. Analyze the market before picking the stocks

This is where it all starts with picking the right stocks. Warren Buffet said, " If you're right about what, you don't have to worry about when." If you do a thorough analysis of the market and you choose the right stocks for your swing trading, chances are that you will do well. But the challenge is how to pick the right stocks for your swing trading. This is where technical analysis and technical indicators come in.

2. Make sure that the market is moving in your prediction

The best strategy is to always look for stocks that are on an upward swing, then looking for sell signals to sell off your position to make a profit. Some people simply get excited about owning a particular stock, they develop an affinity for the stock and fail to sell the stock to take on profit when they have to, even though they claim they are in swing trading. When you are a swing trader, your goal is to buy stocks low and then sell high a couple of weeks to make money.

3. Check the industry and make sure it also has an upward trend

Most companies in the same industry experience the same upward movement. Therefore, if you are looking for technology companies in the same sector, you can look at other related or competitive companies to check whether they are also experiencing an upward swing. This will pre-inform you about the market and make the right strategy swing trading move to capture the profit in the sector.

4. Look for Buy Signals Before You Buy

Just because a market is moving up does not mean you should jump into the trade. Always use the technical indicators such as simple moving averages, candlesticks, support & resistance trigger and trend lines to check whether the market is favorable to buy an underlying financial instrument. Buying at the right time and selling at the right time is the key to successful swing trading.

5. Use technical analysis an back it with fundamental analysis

Technical analysis is the best way to analyze securities and know whether to buy or sell them. While you can use technical indicators to place trades and grow your position, you have to keep watch of the fundamental news. Often times, stock charts, patterns and trends in the financial market are just a reflection of fundamental occurrences in the underlying company. Therefore, find the fundamental facts to support your technical analysis before engaging in a trade.

6. Don't commit too much money to any trade

Stay conservative in any trade. Don't bank your full trust in any trade. It is better to earn 20 % to 25% of every single trade than to be looking at the big lucky break. Evaluate your position and make sure you manage your risk when placing a trade. If you have some few hundred bucks in your trading account, you don't want to commit more than 10% to speculative trading activities. Keep a close eye on the downsides.

7. Set your stop-loss close by

If you the market couldn't go in your favor, you don't have to worry and fret. All you have to do is stop the loss by selling your position and then move to the next thing. You should not agonize over a single loss in swing trading. Learn from it and move to the next thing. Place emergency stop-loss orders to ensure that you don't blow your entire trading account through a single swing trading loss.

5 Questions to Ask Yourself Before You Place a Trade

As a matter of fact, you want to find ways to manage your risk. There's always an amount of risk in swing trading so don't be afraid of taking a risk. What you need to do is to find a way to manage your risk and keep moving forward in the game. Before you place a trade, you need to ask yourself a couple of question to make sure you have done your due diligence and know what you are doing.

The following are the top questions you should ask yourself before placing any trade:

1. Is the security of a high volume and liquid?

Demand for financial instrument tends to increase the underlying price. You want to make sure the security you are trading is a highly liquid and of a very high volume. This ensures that your risk wave is well-positioned to increase your potential of making a hit.

2. Is the security volatile or sedate?

The volatility of security is very important to know whether they are most likely to swing upward or downward in order to make a profit. You don't want to be trading in stocks that are stable, inert and sedate. This is very important when you are trading options. You'll end up having your options expiring worthless because of less volatility of the stock.

3. Is the security a high priced stock or penny stock?

Usually, high priced stocks are expensive to buy and have high risks if the market does not go in your favor. For example, buying 100 shares of ABC selling at $ 250 per share will mean spending $ 25, 000 in the trade. But buying the same 100 shares of XYZ at $ 25 per share will mean spending only $ 2500. What many traders do is to use options trading to buy highly-priced stocks, paying only the premium amount for the option with the contract at a strike price.

4. Have you set a limit to losses of your total portfolio?

You need to set a limit to your losses while engaging in swing trading. This is a great step forward to ensure that you protect your entire portfolio from being drained in the marketed. You can decide to limit the losses of your position to at least 10% of your total portfolio. That means you don't want to expose all of your portfolios to losses in the swing trading.

5. Have you diversified your portfolio?

Diversification is very important in swing trading. What you don't want to do is sink your entire money into a single area.

Consider learning and educating yourself with other areas of investment. Just because you have to diversify does not mean to do what you don't understand. Trade-in markets you understand and are comfortable with. Look at different sectors, different asset classes and ranges of market capitalizations to diversify and expand your portfolio.

Mistakes to Avoid In Swing Trading

1. Avoid Losing Your Cool

We are creatures of habit and emotions. Trading is a mental game, as such, you need to learn to control your emotions of you really want to do well. This is very important because being carried away by emotions of fear and greed can make you lose much further than you think. You should control your emotions and resist the urge to act on impulse.

2. Avoid losing touch with the market analysis

Once you take charge of your emotions, the next thing you want to do is to make sure you are to start with the analysis. Don't think you know it all because you were successful in a previous trade with a certain type of stock. Try your best to exercise patience and then start using the stock charts and the news to evaluate the market before making a trade.

3. Avoid following the masses without proper analysis

Benjamin Graham said, "You're not right because a thousand people agree with you. You're not right because a thousand people disagree with you. You're right because your facts and reasoning are right." Don't follow the masses. Always do your individual analysis and make trade decisions based on clearly thought technical and fundamental indicators of the market.

Conclusion

Thank for making it through to the end of *Swing Trading for Beginners: How to Become a Swing Trader with Strategies, Routines, Tools. Technical Analysis for Stocks, Options and Forex Investments, Trading Psychology and Money Management*, let's hope it was informative and able to provide you with all of the tools you need to achieve your goals, whatever it is that they may be. Just because you've finished this book, doesn't mean there is nothing left to learn on the topic, expanding your horizons is the only way to find the mastery you seek. What's more, to be a truly successful trader is to be a lifelong learner as the nature of the market is always in flux which means that there will always be new strategies coming into existence to take advantage of that fact.

The next step is to stop reading already and to get ready to get started taking advantage of the benefits that are unique to a swing trading strategy. While it may not be exciting, what this means in practical terms is that it is time for you to get down to business and start doing your homework. While you might want to avoid all of that and jump right in, as previously mentioned all this is likely to do is to nip your trading career in the bud before it even begins.

The game of swing trading is a mental game. Therefore, above the technical skills and experience, you need to succeed, you need to make sure you exhibit the right attitudes. As they say, " attitude is everything." If you put forth the right attitude and learn the tricks of the game, you will do well that those who do not.

Be conservative. While you can make huge profits in swing trading, avoid the "get rich quick" attitude. Don't be lured by the success stories of those swing traders who buy big houses, big boats and go for amazing vacations through their income from swing trading. Success takes time, dedication and experience.

Another thing you have to take note of is your mindset. There are many success stories of people who are making it swing trading. Avoid dealing with negative, bitter people who have been hurt in the trade, Remember that that you will become who you associate with. Therefore, associated yourself with seasoned, experienced and successful swing trader in every financial market and learn their mindset. There's always something to learn every day to get better in the game of swing trading.

You can always learn from your mistakes as well as other people's mistakes. Just know that every trade you place is a learning experience. The more you learn from trading mistakes and fine-tune your trading strategy, the better off you will be in swing trading. Always evaluate your trade and learn something new from the experience.

Start using tools such as candlesticks, stock charts, and many others to make better trading predictions. The fact is that the better your predictions and analysis, the better your swing trading results will be. All I require is practice over a period of time. When you begin to practice using the tools of technical analysis in stock trend prediction, you will become better at and get better results.

Finally, if you found this book useful in any way, a review on Amazon is always appreciated!

www.ingramcontent.com/pod-product-compliance
Lightning Source LLC
Chambersburg PA
CBHW070352220526
45467CB00001B/345